Visual Search

SYMPOSIUM CONDUCTED AT
THE SPRING MEETING, 1970

COMMITTEE ON VISION
DIVISION OF BEHAVIORAL SCIENCES
NATIONAL RESEARCH COUNCIL

NATIONAL ACADEMY OF SCIENCES
WASHINGTON, D.C.
1973

Reproduction is sponsored by Contract N00014-67-A-0244-0211 between the National Research Research Council Committee on Vision and the Office of Naval Research.

LIBRARY OF CONGRESS CATALOGING IN PUBLICATION DATA
Main entry under title:

Visual search.

Includes bibliographies.
1. Visual perception—Congresses. I. National Research Council. Division of Behavioral Sciences. Committee on Vision. [DNLM: 1. Vision—Congresses. WW 103 N277v 1970]
BF241.V57   152.1'4   72-10766
ISBN 0-309-02103-0

BF
241
V57
1973

Available from
Printing and Publishing Office, National Academy of Sciences
2101 Constitution Avenue, N.W., Washington, D.C.   20418

Printed in the United States of America

Preface

In 1959, the Committee on Vision sponsored a symposium on visual search. Continued interest in this subject prompted the Committee to sponsor another symposium to survey theoretical and experimental developments during the past 10 years since the publication of the proceedings of the 1959 symposium.

The papers in this volume were presented at the Committee's annual meeting in May 1970.

Contents

JOHN R. BLOOMFIELD
UNIVERSITY OF NOTTINGHAM

Experiments in Visual Search

I shall describe briefly some of the findings obtained in a continuing study of visual search conducted at the University of Nottingham.

Gottsdanker (1960) listed some of the many factors involved in search. One search determinant that he isolated, the competition determinant, refers to the situation in which a target is clearly distinguishable from its immediate background but is difficult to detect because it can be confused with other nontarget stimuli that are also present in the search area. The problem is one of discrimination, and, obviously, the greater the degree of similarity of the target and the nontargets, the harder the task will be. The target may differ with respect to one or more of the following dimensions: color, contrast, shape, and size. Other variables that must be considered, some of which are interrelated, are heterogeneity, number, density and distribution of the nontargets, and size of the search area.

The effects of shape alone and effects of contrast and size in combination with shape were investigated by Smith (1961, 1962). In the first group of experiments on the effect of competition on search, the targets differed only in size.

The apparatus was designed so that observers could be tested repeatedly. Repeated testing is not possible if only a small set of the apparently possible target positions are used, for observers would be able to learn the limited set of positions actually used, to make use

1

of this information, and, thus, to reduce the time they need to locate the target. In studies in which a small number of stimulus cards have been used (Eriksen, 1955; Green and Anderson, 1956; McGill, 1960), it has been necessary to pool data from untrained observers. Pooled data can give an indication of the effect of the variables involved, but it may also obscure some effects. In the tasks used here, all apparently possible target positions were actually possible, and the observers could be repeatedly tested. The apparatus proved readily adaptable, and a series of related experiments were undertaken.

APPARATUS AND GENERAL PROCEDURE

The search displays were Perspex sheets with shallow holes drilled in predetermined positions in their surfaces. Ball bearings of various sizes could be placed in the indentations and the displays masked off to give a search area of the required shape and size. The sheets were placed on an overhead projector and projected onto a screen. Target position could be changed rapidly from one presentation to the next, in accordance with a previously determined random order. The number of positions that the target could occupy was limited only by the total number of stimulus positions in the display. The observer was asked to find the target as quickly as possible. He was seated in front of the display and behind a shutter. The arrangement for projection is shown diagramatically in Figure 1. When ready, the observer opened the shutter, looked for the target, and, as soon as he located it, closed the shutter. The length of time the shutter was opened was recorded automatically. The observer indicated verbally where he thought the target was after the shutter had been closed.

The observer sat 9 ft away from the screen. At this distance, the square displays used in the experiments reported here were approximately 16°20' on each side. Their actual length was 4.5 in. unprojected and approximately 2 ft 7.5 in. when projected. Two square displays were used. One contained 100 indentations, arranged regularly in a 10 × 10 matrix. For the second, one third of the 324 intersections of an 18 × 18 matrix were selected at random to give a 108 position irregular display. The two displays are shown in Figure 2. The diameter and area of each of the seven disks used as target and nontarget stimuli are shown in Table 1.

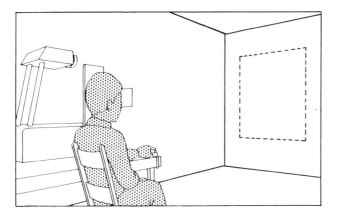

FIGURE 1   Sketch of experimental arrangement showing
overhead projector, shutter, response key, screen, and the
position of the observer.

All seven stimuli could be used with the regular display but only
the smaller four (A–D) with the irregular display. After a run of ten
consecutive search trials with a given target, the observer had a short
rest. Experimental sessions were just under 1 hr in length and consisted of six such runs.

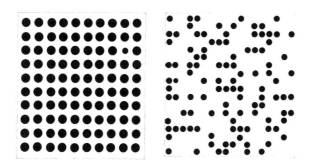

FIGURE 2   Regular and irregular search displays each
containing a target disk slightly smaller than the background stimuli.

TABLE 1   Diameter and Area of Stimulus Disks

Discs	A	B	C	D	E	F	10
Unprojected diameter (32nds of inch)	4	5	6	7	8	9	–
Projected diameter (min of arc)	27.2	34.0	40.8	47.6	54.4	61.2	68.0
Projected area (sq. min)	581	908	1,308	1,779	2,325	2,943	3,632

RESULTS

Size Differences between Target Disk and Surrounding Disks

The effect of varying the differences in size of a target disk and the nontargets has been investigated for both regular and irregular displays (Bloomfield, 1969). Search data are often reported in terms of mean or median times. Figure 3 shows the frequency distributions of times needed to locate the six targets, A to F, with stimuli of size G as nontargets, for one observer ($S1$). The figure shows that, as the difference in size of the target and nontargets decreases, the distributions increase in variability and range and become increasingly skewed, as well as having their means and medians increase. Much of this information can be preserved by presenting the data in the form of cumulative distributions for three observers ($S1, S2, S3$) with normal vision (one corrected) searching the regular display (the data of Figure 3 are replotted on Figure 4a). Similarly, Figure 5 shows data from the same three observers for the irregular display. It should be noted that the origins of the cumulative curves do not coincide and that none of them passes through the origin of the graph.

Search is only necessary when, for some reason, a target cannot be located immediately. If a target is perceptually prominent in a particular display, varying its position in that display will have little effect; the range of location times obtained for it will be very small, and the cumulative distribution of these times should be steep.

The point on the continuum of size-differences between target and nontargets at which search becomes necessary is within the range of differences used with the regular display. The distributions for the

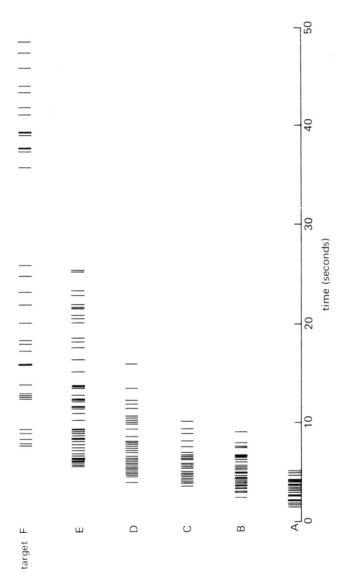

FIGURE 3 Frequency distributions for targets A–F in the regular display, $S1$ (distribution for F continues up to 43.70 sec).

5

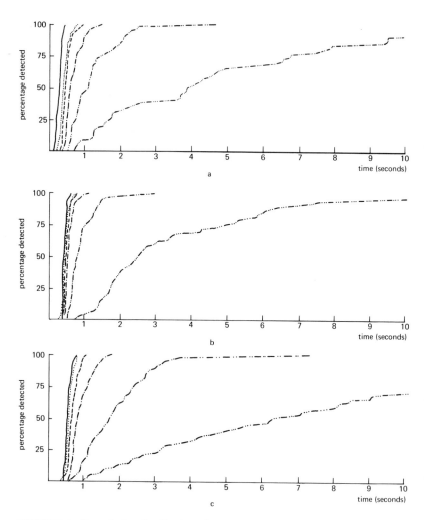

FIGURE 4   Cumulative distributions for targets A–F in the regular display of
background stimuli G: 60 readings per distribution. (a) *S*1, (b) *S*2, (c) *S*3.
_____A, ...B, - - - - - - -C, -.-.-.-.-.D, -..-..-..-..-..E, -...-...-...-...-...F.

targets most different in size from the background stimuli (A, B, C
for *S*1 and *S*2; B for *S*3) are very steep, suggesting that little or no
search was necessary to locate them. The times obtained are perhaps
best considered as response times that have two components, a reaction time dependent on how efficiently the observer can manipulate

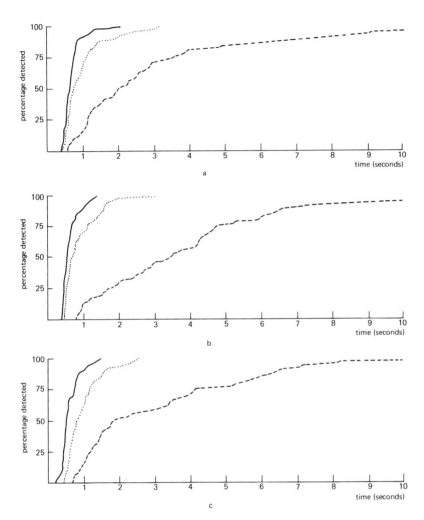

FIGURE 5   Cumulative distributions for targets A–C in the irregular display of background stimuli D: 60 readings per distribution. (a) $S1$, (b) $S2$, (c) $S3$. _____A, ...B, - - - - -C.

the shutter and a processing time in which he decides whether he can see the target. The distributions of the remaining targets appear to be increasingly dependent on search factors, as well as containing elements of response factors. For middle-range size differences (D for $S1$; D, E for $S2$; C, D for $S3$) the distributions are fairly steep at first, and then, later, have a more gradual incline. Probably for these targets most of the display can be covered in one or two fixations, with a few target positions toward the boundary requiring more. For the targets closest in size to the nontargets (E, F for $S1$ and $S3$; F for S2), the time distributions have more gradual slopes. Many fixations are needed on most trials with these targets.

With the irregular display, all three targets seem to have required search to some extent. Again as the similarity between the target and nontarget increases, the distributions appear to be increasingly dependent on search factors.

Fitting Exponentials

Krendel and Wodinsky (1960a,b) reported an extensive study in which search times were obtained for targets of varying contrast and size located in otherwise completely featureless backgrounds. They were able able to describe quite adequately much of their data by exponential equations of the form

$$P_T = 1 - (1 - p_s)^{\frac{T}{t_s}} ,$$

where P_T is the probability of locating a target by time T, p_s the probability of detecting a target in a single fixation, and t_s the average time for a fixation. Several theoretical approaches to search (Krendel and Wodinsky, 1960a,b; Lamar, 1960; McGill, 1960; Davies, 1968; Howarth and Bloomfield, 1968, 1969) have incorporated the suggestion that search times should be exponentially distributed. In Figures 6 and 7, the data of Figures 4 and 5 are replotted on semilog scales as $1 - P_T$, rather than P_T, against time. If the distributions are exponential, they should fall on straight lines when plotted in this way. Straight lines, fitted by eye, are included on both figures. The distributions are shown only for those targets that seemed to have required search: For the regular display, targets A, B, and C are omitted for $S1$ and $S2$, and A and B are omitted for $S3$. The data can be seen to fit least well for the targets nearest in size to the nontargets, i.e., for those more dependent on search factors. Again it should be noted that the distributions neither pass through the origin of the graphs nor have a common origin, as the previously mentioned theoretical treatments suggest they should.

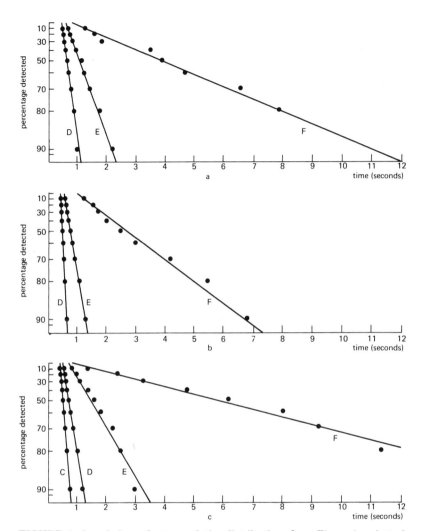

FIGURE 6   Search-dependent cumulative distributions from Figure 4 replotted on semilog coordinates. (a) $S1$, (b) $S2$, (c) $S3$.

Numbers and Density Nontargets

The three variables, density of nontargets, number of nontargets, and size of the search area, are inextricably bound up. One can be held constant while the other two are varied, but the converse is not true. Thus, all findings in search experiments purporting to investigate one of these variables can, in fact, be attributed to two possible sources

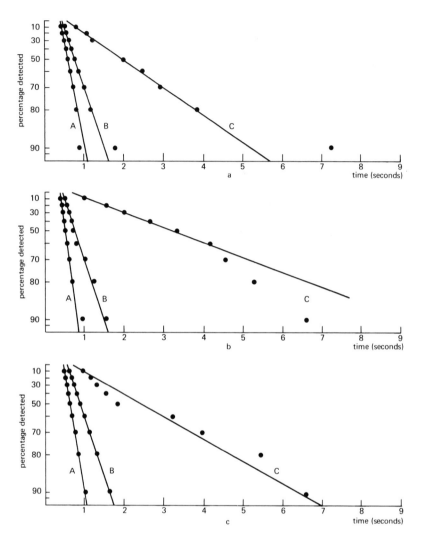

FIGURE 7   Cumulative distributions from Figure 5 replotted on semilog coordinates. (a) $S1$, (b) $S2$, (c) $S3$.

of variation. It is surprising that in this area, which has proved most
attractive to those using competition search tasks, this has not always
been made clear.

The general findings are that increasing number with density (area
constant) or number with area (density constant) increases search

time. The third possibility, holding number constant and increasing density by reducing area, has received little attention; Eriksen's (1955) results were inconsistent and probably artifactual, while Baker *et al.* (1960) found no changes in search time when density was varied in this way.

The relation between mean or median time and number and density or number and area appeared, in some studies, to be roughly linear. However, Smith (1961) showed the relationship was more complex. He suggested that

$$t = a\,N^{\mathrm{m}},$$

where t is search time, N the number of nontargets, and a and m are constants. This power function was not adequate for his data obtained with targets differing on two or three dimensions. However, it did seem appropriate for data obtained when only one dimension was involved. In fact, m often had a value close to .50, suggesting a square root relationship between N and t.

Using the apparatus already described, this relation was investigated further. A regular 7 × 7 display was used as low density, with the 10 × 10 regular display of Figure 2 as high density. One practiced observer, $S6$, was used. The nontargets were of size D, and there were three smaller (A, B, C) and three larger targets (E, F, G). The 12 display-target conditions were randomized.

The results are shown in Figure 8. For all six targets there was a marked reduction in search time for the low-density display. The semilog plot gives further evidence that exponential functions provide good descriptions of search data. In addition, strong support is provided for the proposed square root relation between search time and the number of nontargets. The lines shown for each target-density condition are related as follows:

$$\frac{G_L}{\sqrt{N_L}} = \frac{G_H}{\sqrt{N_H}},$$

where G_L and G_H are the gradients of lines for the low and high densities, and N_L and N_H are the number of stimuli in the low- and high-density displays. The pairs of lines were fitted by eye. The square root relationship appears to hold over the complete distributions.

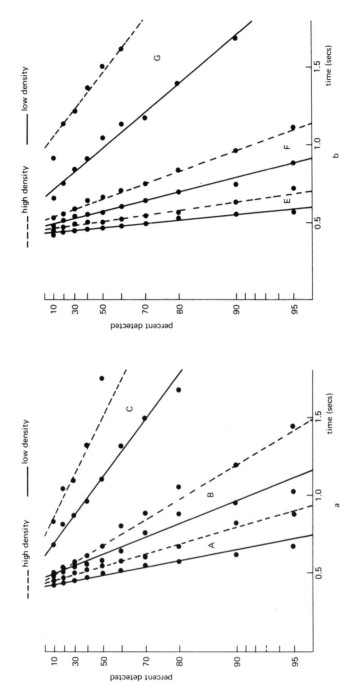

FIGURE 8 Semilog plot of cumulative distributions based on 60 readings, for (a) targets A–C (b) targets E–G in high and low density regular displays, with D as nontargets.

Relating Search Time to Target-Background Characteristics

It has been traditional, since Wertheim (1894), to refer to peripheral
acuity in terms of the reciprocal of the angular measure of a threshold stimulus. Low (1951) pointed out that this led to the erroneous
view that acuity decreases rapidly at first and then more slowly as the
far periphery is reached. In fact, the decrease is virtually linear until
the far periphery and then is more rapid. Weymouth (1958) pointed
out that a linear relation holds from the fovea out to 20° or 30° for
a wide range of threshold data. Howarth and Bloomfield (1968, 1969)
and Bloomfield and Howarth (1969) made use of this linearity and of
basic search theory in deriving the following relation:

$$\bar{t} \propto \frac{1}{(d_B - d_T)^2} \, , \tag{1}$$

where $\bar{t}$ is mean search time, and d_B and d_T the diameters of the background and target stimuli.

   This was found to describe some of the previously obtained data.
Figure 9 replots data of $S1$ and $S3$ from Figure 4, and Figure 10

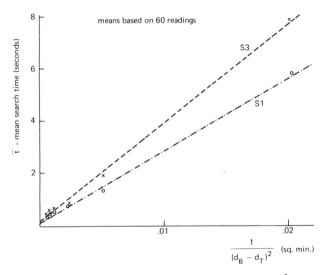

FIGURE 9   The relationship between $\bar{t}$ and $1/(d_B - d_T)^2$ for
two subjects searching a regularly arranged display with the
largest disks as nontargets.

John R. Bloomfield

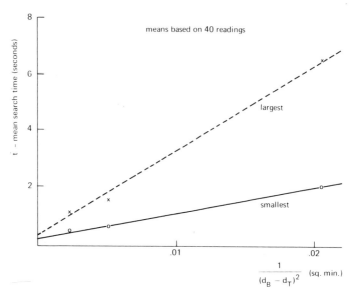

FIGURE 10   The relationship between $\bar{t}$ and $1/(d_B\text{-}d_T)^2$ for one
subject searching an irregularly arranged display with, in one case,
the largest disks and, in the other, the smallest as nontargets.

shows the relationship for a further observer, *S*5, searching the irregular display with targets larger (B, C, D with nontargets A) or
smaller (A, B, C with nontargets D) than the background stimuli.

To deal with threshold search, in which a low contrast target is
embedded in a plain background, Howarth and Bloomfield (1968)
extracted the relationship between target size and eccentricity from
the peripheral acuity data of Taylor (1961). The derived a very similar relation for threshold search situations:

$$\bar{t} \ \propto \ \frac{1}{(d_T - d_0)^2} \ ,$$

where d_0 is the threshold diameter of a target at the fovea.

The adequacy of this relation is shown in Figures 11 and 12. The
data used in Figure 11 are from Miller and Ludvigh (1960). The value
of d_0 has been taken as 5.0', although we have no direct information
on this variable in this experiment. However, a direct estimate was
made for Figure 12. The data were obtained by G. Hill with one prac-

ticed observer (*S22*). The diameters of the disk targets were 6.7′, 8.0′, 10.7′, and 13.3′; the search display was 14°35′ square, and d_0 was 3.65′.

Relating Response Time to Target-Background Characteristics

As pointed out earlier, the cumulative time distributions do not pass through any common origin in Figures 4, 5, 6, 7, and 8. The origins of the distributions can be considered as the response times required by the observers to respond to the presence of a target with no element of search. This would occur when the observer is able to detect the target with his first glimpse of the display. The fastest time, t_f, obtained over a set of search trials with a particular target can be taken as an estimate of response time. This is only a crude estimate. However, it is found that the average t_f for *S1*, *S2*, and *S3* for the data shown in Figures 4 and 5 can be related not to the square of the

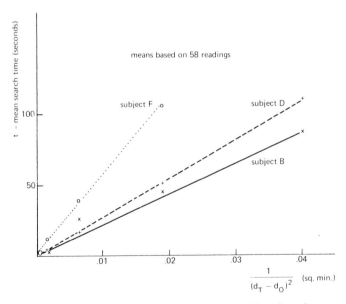

FIGURE 11   Data from Miller and Ludvigh (1960) replotted to show the relationship between $\bar{t}$ and $1/(d_T - d_0)^2$ for search in a plain background—assuming $d = t$ min of arc.

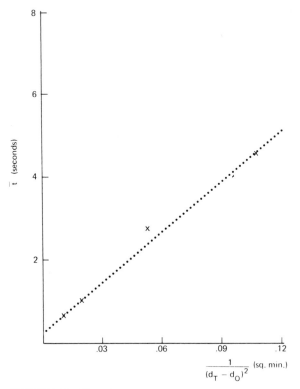

FIGURE 12   The relationship between mean search time
and the reciprocal of $(d_T - d_0)^2$ for search in a plain background.

diameter difference of target and background disks but to the diameter difference itself, thus:

$$t_f \propto \frac{1}{|d_B - d_T|} \cdot \tag{2}$$

This is illustrated in Figure 13. The method of least squares was used
to obtain the lines of best fit added to the figure. For the regular display, 99.6 percent and, for the irregular, 99.36 percent of the vari-
ances are accounted for by the simple diameter difference relation.

   Unlike relation (1), there was no theoretical derivation of relation
(2), and at least one other function, derived from Crossman (1955),
provides as good a fit to the data. [This function is $t_f \propto 1/(\log d_B - \log d_T)$.]

An Index of Target Difficulty

A basic problem in many search situations occurs when an attempt is made to specify the properties of a background that relate to the difficulty of locating a particular target. Often there is no metric for the necessary specification. In the competition search experiments described so far, the difference between targets and nontargets was size, and it could be measured precisely. Possibly other target-background complexes could be treated in terms of size measures, if use is made of relations (1) and (2). This can be illustrated in treating the data of two further experiments. In the first of these, carried out by R. D. Wright, two or three targets were presented in the display adjacent to each other. In the second, carried out by D. M. Donnelly, targets of varying shape were employed. In both experiments, the basic procedure was as already described, the

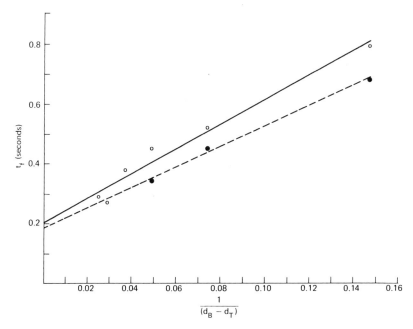

FIGURE 13   Relation between t_f and the reciprocal of $(d_B - d_T)$: t_f averaged over three observers. ∘——∘ regular display, line of best fit $t_f = .204 + (4.09)/(d_B - d_T)$; •——• irregular display, line of best fit $t_f = .184 + (3.41)/(d_B - d_T)$.

regular display of Figure 2 was used, and the nontargets were of size G.

In the multiple target experiment, two or three targets of size F were positioned on the display, either grouped adjacent to each other or dispersed at random throughout the display, and the observer (*S*23) was asked to locate one of them as quickly as possible. There were also two standard conditions in which single targets of sizes E and F were present. Figure 14 shows the cumulative distributions based on 60 trials for each of the six target conditions. The two triple target conditions result in faster times than the double targets, and all four multiple target conditions lay between the distributions of targets E and F alone. The grouped targets are found more quickly than the first of the comparable multiple targets placed at random. As expected, the randomly placed targets share a common origin with the stardard target F, while the grouped targets do not.

On Figure 15, the mean search times for the the two standard targets were plotted as a function of the reciprocal of the square of the target-background diameter difference. A linear relation (1) was assumed for these two targets, and the mean times for the two

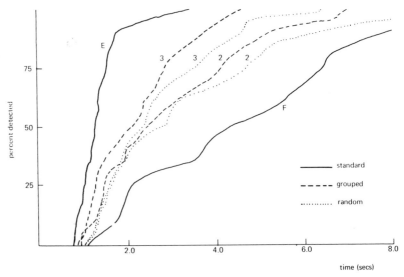

FIGURE 14   Cumulative distributions, based on 60 readings, for standard (E and F), grouped (2 and 3), and random (2 and 3) targets.

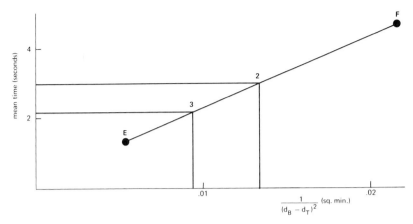

FIGURE 15 The relationship between mean search time and $1/(d_B - d_T)^2$ for the standard targets (E and F) used to derive apparent diameter differences for grouped targets (2 and 3).

grouped targets were used to read off apparent values of $1/(d_B - d_T)^2$. From these, $1/(d_B - d_T)$ could be derived. Figure 16 shows the plot of fastest time against the $1/(d_B - d_T)$ values of E and F, with the expected linear relation (2) drawn in. The derived values for the grouped targets are also shown.

In the second experiment, there were four differently shaped targets: 4, a square, 3.2 percent larger than disk F; 6, a hexagon, 4.5 percent smaller; 8, an octagon, 1.6 percent smaller; and 12, a duodecagon, 6.0 percent larger. These targets were made of stiff opaque paper. Each was mounted on a dressmaking pin. A small nut provided a firm base with the pin head resting in one of the indentations in the Perspex display sheet. Again targets E and F were used as standards, and there was one observer ($S24$). Figure 17 shows the cumulative distributions based on 60 trials for each of the six target conditions. As the shaped targets become more like disks, going from square through hexagon and octagon to duodecagon, more time is required to locate them among the nontarget disks (which are of size G). The octagon and target E have distributions that are not significantly different from each other.

On Figure 18, as before, mean times were plotted as a function of $1/(d_B - d_T)^2$, linear relation (1) assumed, and then apparent diameter

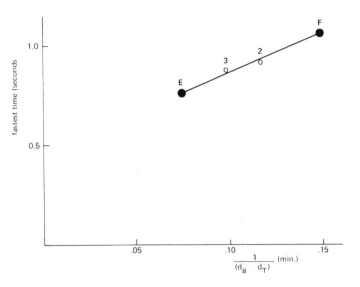

FIGURE 16   The relationship between fastest search time and
$1/(d_B - d_T)$ for the standard (E and F) and grouped (2 and 3) targets,
using the apparent diameters derived in Figure 15.

values were read off for the four shapes. These values could be used
for comparison with the relation (2) for the standard targets, as on
Figure 19. The line of best fit for the shapes is not significantly different from the standard line.

In the case of both the grouped and the differently shaped targets,
the values derived from relations (1) and (2) agree fairly well. Since
the octagon and standard target E have similar means and fastest
times as well as distributions, a further test of the proposed metric is
suggested. This would involve a comparison of search times for a target of size G in (a) nontargets of size E and in (b) octagon-shaped
nontargets. If the resulting distributions were very close, it would
seem feasible that a scale for shape could be obtained. This procedure
is not possible for grouped targets, nor could it be used in many more
complicated situations. However, there is hope that a range of target-
background complexes could be handled numerically by treating
them on an apparent diameter difference scale.

While one may be cautiously optimistic, this approach is obviously
limited. It is doubtful if it could be used in camouflage situations,

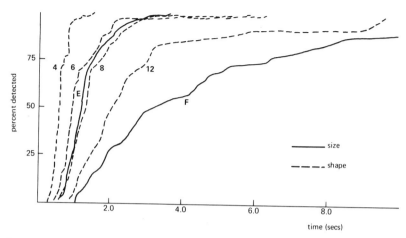

FIGURE 17 Cumulative distributions for standard (E and F) and shape (4–square, 6–hexagon, 8–octagon, 12–duodecagon) targets.

where the target fails to emerge perceptually from its immediate background because the patterning of the background and target combine to obscure the latter. Although of major importance, problems of camouflage have received little systematic investigation. This is due, in part, to the great difficulties in defining camouflage situa-

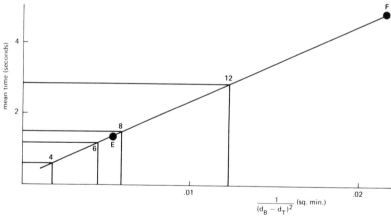

FIGURE 18 The relationship between mean search time and $1/(d_B - d_T)^2$ for the standard targets (E and F) used to derive apparent diameter differences for shape targets (4, 6, 8, and 12).

John R. Bloomfield

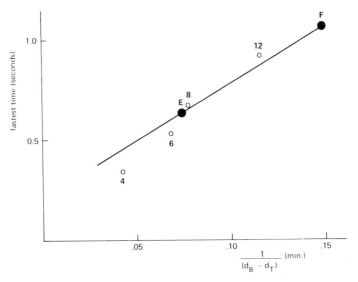

FIGURE 19   The relationship between fastest search time and
$1/(d_B - d_T)$ for the standard (E and F) and grouped (2 and 3)
targets using the apparent diameters derived in Figure 18.

tions. Figure 20 illustrates some of the problems. In this collection
of triangles and quadrilaterals, there is embedded a regular five-
pointed star. It is not clear exactly what the relevant variables are
in this task. While it is possible to make quite precise theoretical
statements about the artificial stimuli used in competition search

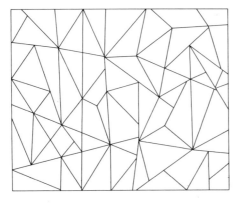

FIGURE 20   A camouflage search
task; find the five-pointed star.

tasks, we are still a very long way from being able to deal with the kind of complexities involved in camouflage situations.

SUMMARY

The work described here was carried out in an attempt to elucidate some of the problems involved in visual search. There were two general objectives: (1) to provide a sound body of empirical data and (2) to develop a viable theoretical framework.

Several experiments have been performed with competition search tasks in which the target had to be located when other nontarget stimuli were also present in the display. An adaptable apparatus was devised. This enabled a series of studies to be undertaken, some of which are reported here. It was found that as the difference in size of targets and nontargets decreased search times increased for both regularly arranged and irregularly arranged stimulus displays. For some easier targets, the location times were largely dependent on response factors, while the times became more and more dependent on search factors as the target–nontarget difference decreased. A comparison of two display densities led to the suggestion that search time is a function of the square root of the number and density of nontargets. Search times appear to be distributed exponentially.

Howarth and Bloomfield (1968, 1969) derived a model of search that makes use of the linear relationship between threshold stimulus size and retinal eccentricity. Using this model, it is possible to relate mean search times to target-background characteristics, in particular to the square of the difference in diameter of target and nontarget discs. This approach is illustrated here. It is argued that the fastest search time obtained for a given target can be taken as an estimate of response time. This time is not related to the square of the diameter difference but to the difference itself. It is suggested that these two relations, of mean search time and fastest search time with target-background characteristics, might be used to develop a measure in terms of diameter differences for search situations in which the target and background differ in other ways than size. This is illustrated for grouped targets and targets differing in shape.

While some progress has been made, we remain a long way from being able to deal with many complex search situations.

24 *John R. Bloomfield*

ACKNOWLEDGMENTS

This work is supported by a contract between the Ministry of Aviation Supply (formerly Ministry of Technology) and the Department of Psychology, University of Nottingham, U.K. A complete description of the work is given in Bloomfield (1970). Thanks are due to Professor C. I. Howarth, who supervised this work and with whom I collaborated on the theoretical model, and B. Hill, R. D. Wright, and D. M. Donnelly, who carried out some of the experiments.

REFERENCES

Baker, C. A., D. F. Morris, and W. C. Steedman. Target recognition on complex displays. Hum. Factors, 2, 51–61, 1960.

Bloomfield, J. R. Visual search. The effect of systematically varying the difference in size of target and nontarget background stimuli. In H. W. Leibowitz, ed., NATO Symposium on Image Evaluation, 1969.

Bloomfield, J. R. Visual search. PhD Thesis. University of Nottingham, 1970.

Bloomfield, J. R., and C. I. Howarth. Testing visual search theory. In H. W. Leibowitz, ed., NATO Symposium on Image Evaluation, 1969.

Crossman, E. R. F. W. The measurement of discriminability. Q. J. Exp. Psych., 7, 176–195, 1955.

Davies, E. B. Visual theory in target acquisition. In AGARD Conference Proceedings No. 41, A.1, 1968.

Eriksen, C. W. Partitioning and saturation of visual displays and efficiency of visual search. J. Appl. Psych., 39, 73–77, 1955.

Gottsdanker, R. The relation between the nature of the search situation and the effectiveness of alternative strategies of search. In A. Morris, and E. P. Horne, eds., Visual Search Techniques, NAS–NRC Committee on Vision, Washington, D.C., 181–186, 1960.

Green, B. F. and L. K. Anderson. Color coding in a visual search task. Q. J. Exp. Psych., 51, 19–24, 1956.

Howarth, C. I., and J. R. Bloomfield. Towards a theory of visual search. In AGARD Conference Proceedings No. 41, A.2, 1968.

Howarth, C. I., and J. R. Bloomfield. A rational equation for predicting search times in simple inspection tasks. Psychonomic Sci., 17, 225–226, 1969.

Krendel, E. S., and J. Wodinsky. Visual search in unstructured fields. In A. Morris and E. P. Horne, eds., Visual Search Techniques, NAS–NRC Committee on Vision, Washington, D.C., 151–169, 1960a.

Krendel, E. S., and J. Wodinsky. Search in an unstructured visual field. J. Opt. Soc. Am., 50, 562–568, 1960b.

Lamar, E. S. Operational background and physical considerations relative to visual search problems. In A. Morris and E. P. Horne, eds., Visual Search Techniques, NAS–NRC Committee on Vision, Washington, D.C., 1–9, 1960.

Low, F. N. Peripheral visual acuity. Ophthalmol. Rev. Arch. Ophthalmol., 45, 80–99, 1951.

McGill, W. J. Search distributions in magnified time. In A. Morris and E. P. Horne, eds., Visual Search Techniques, NAS–NRC Committee on Vision, Washington, D.C., 50–58, 1960.

Miller, J. W., and E. Ludvigh. Time required for detection of stationary and moving objects as a function of size in homogeneous and partially structured visual fields. In A. Morris and E. P. Horne, eds., Visual Search Techniques, NAS–NRC Committee on Vision, Washington, D.C., 170–180, 1960.

Smith, S. W. Time required for target detection in complex abstract visual display. Memorandum 2900-235-R. Inst. of Science & Technology, University of Michigan, 1961.

Smith, S. W. Problems in the design of sensor output displays. In M. A. Whitcomb, ed., Visual Problems of the Armed Forces, NAS–NRC Committee on Vision, Washington, D.C., 146–157, 1962.

Taylor, J. H. Private communication in Linge. Visual detection from aircraft. General Dynamics/Convair Eng. Res. Rep. ASTIA 270630, 1961.

Wertheim, T. Uber die indirekte Schscharfe. Z. Psych. Physiol. Sinnesorg., 7, 172–187, 1894. Cited in Low (1951).

Weymouth, F. W. Visual sensory units and the minimal angle of resolution. Am. J. Ophthalmol., 41, 102–113, 1958.

JAMES L. HARRIS
SCRIPPS INSTITUTION OF OCEANOGRAPHY

Visual Aspects of Air Collision

When two aircraft are on a possible collision course and one of both of the aircraft is flying under Visual Flight Rules (VFR), then collision avoidance depends upon visual detection of the other aircraft, estimation of the course of the other aircraft, and execution of an avoidance maneuver, if necessary. Visual detection is the first link in this chain of events, for the remaining events cannot occur until detection has occurred. This paper reports research directed toward quantitative evaluation of the visual detection portion of the air-to-air encounter.

The techniques of what is termed visibility engineering have been under development for many years and have been reported (Duntley, 1964). The specific steps followed in the present study are described briefly in the following paragraphs.

Scale models of a DC-3, 737, and a DC-8 were mounted on a post and illuminated with sun, sky, and terrain components. The sun was high and at an azimuth of 135° to the right of the optical axis of the camera. The models were photographed from four aspects: nose-on, ±45° from nose-on, and +90° from nose-on.

The resulting photographic negatives were digitized in a photo-

*This research was supported by Ames Research Center, National Aeronautics and Space Administration.

26

electric film scanner. The scanning aperture takes discrete steps across the film, recording film transmittance at each point. The measurements were made in a square array 64 points on a side (4,096) points in all). Row A in Figures 1, 2, and 3 shows photographs of cathode-ray-tube (CRT) displays of the 64 × 64 arrays for all four aspects of the aircraft.

The remainder of Figures 1, 2, and 3 shows preliminary steps required before calculations could begin. These steps consisted of (B) computer conversion of the negative to a positive (based on the characteristic curve of the film), (C) insertion of a grid to facilitate location of the post, (D) subtraction of the background level to produce a contrast map (negative values are made positive in the display process), (E) elimination of the post, and (F) addition of the background level to reproduce a luminance map.

Taylor's data (1964)—on contrast thresholds in visual search for a stimulus of 1/3 sec duration—were used to derive summative functions (Harris, 1969; Blackwell, 1963). The discrete contrast maps of the aircraft were convolved with these summative functions. The scale of the aircraft was varied to correspond to different distances, and the convolution repeated. The maximum value of this convolution as a function of aircraft range is shown in Figures 4–15. These maximum values are labeled *contrast* since they are dimensionally a contrast. I refer to them as *convolution contrast*. The aircraft have both positive and negative contrast values, and the convolution results in both a positive and negative maximum. Both are plotted in the figures. The horizontal line, labeled $v = \infty$, corresponds to a 50 percent threshold; that is, the probability of detection will be .5 where the horizontal line intersects the peak convolution contrast curve for a single 1/3-sec fixation.

At threshold range, the aircraft will appear to have one contrast polarity. For example, we see in Figure 4 that the aircraft is liminally detectable at approximately 10 nautical miles as a negative contrast (darker than the background), and we can further see that at that range the positive contrast portion of the aircraft is far below threshold.

Since, for horizontal viewing through a horizontally stratified atmosphere, the contrast of an object is attenuated exponentially with range, straight lines corresponding to selected meteorological ranges

28   *James L. Harris*

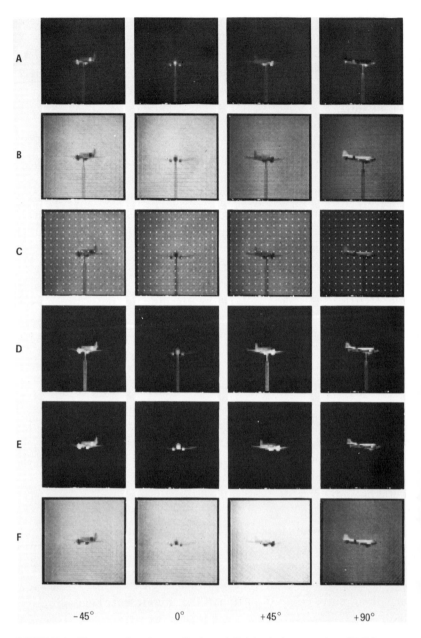

FIGURE 1   Photographs of C R T display of digitized photographs of DC-3
model. Columns are different aspects of the same model, and rows are successive stages of computer processing (see text).

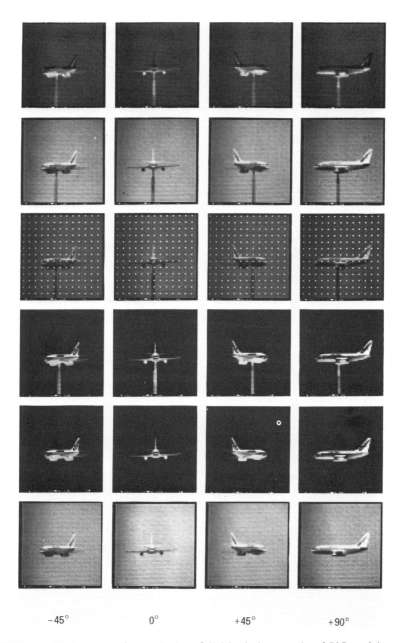

FIGURE 2 Photographs of CRT display of digitized photographs of 737 model. Columns are different aspects of the same model, and rows are successive stages of computer processing (see text).

　　　　　　　　　　　　　　　　　　　　　James L. Harris

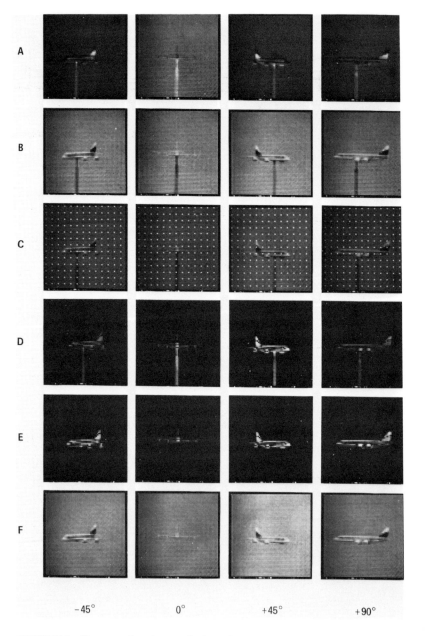

FIGURE 3   Photographs of CRT display of digitized photographs of DC-8 model. Columns are different aspects of the same model, and rows are successive stages of computer processing (see text).

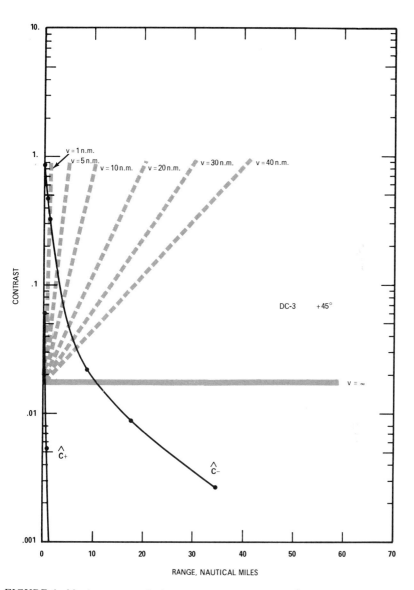

FIGURE 4   Maximum convolution contrast of DC-3 at +45° aspect as a function of range. Maximum positive and negative contrasts are ĉ+ and ĉ–. Functions labeled v are atmospheric visibility conditions in nautical miles ($v = \infty$ means no atmospheric attenuation). Intersection of v and $\hat{c}$ indicates .5 probability of detection.

James L. Harris

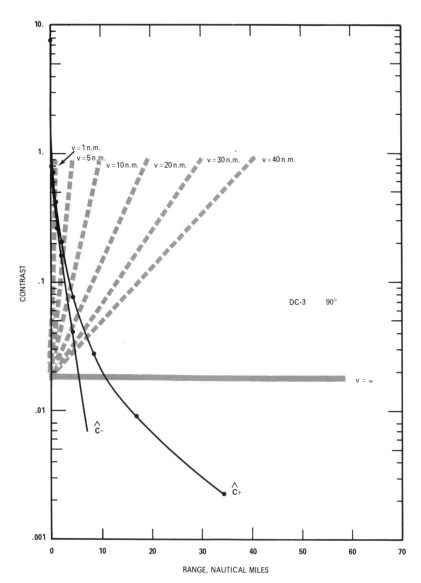

FIGURE 5 Maximum convolution contrast of DC-3 at 90° aspect as a function of range. Maximum positive and negative contrasts are ĉ+ and ĉ–. Functions labeled v are atmospheric visibility conditions in nautical miles ($v = \infty$ means no atmospheric attenuation). Intersection of v and ĉ indicates .5 probability of detection.

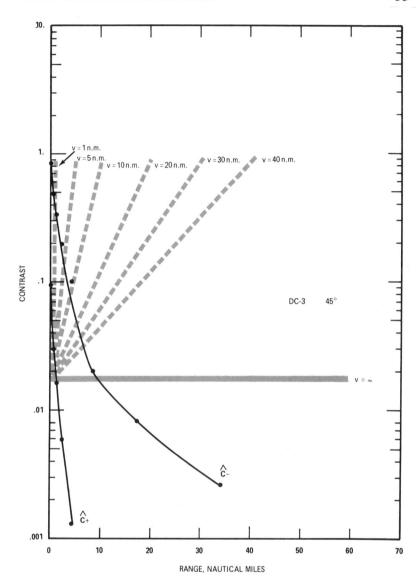

FIGURE 6   Maximum convolution contrast of DC-3 at 45° aspect as a function
of range. Maximum positive and negative contrasts are $\hat{c}+$ and $\hat{c}-$. Functions labeled v are atmospheric visibility conditions in nautical miles ($v = \infty$ means no
atmospheric attenuation). Intersection of v and $\hat{c}$ indicates .5 probability of detection.

James L. Harris

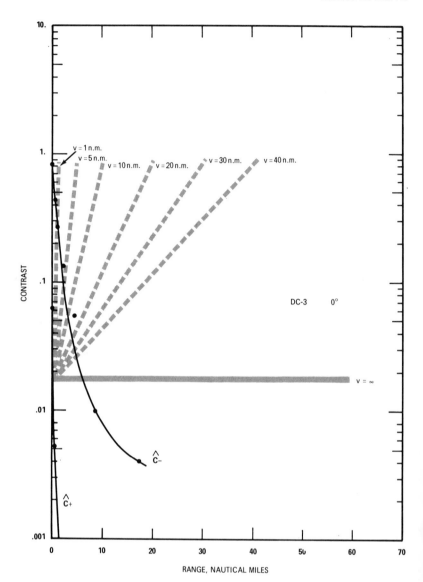

FIGURE 7   Maximum convolution contrast of DC-3 at $0°$ aspect as a function
of range. Maximum positive and negative contrasts are $\hat{c}+$ and $\hat{c}-$. Functions labeled v are atmospheric visibility conditions in nautical miles ($v = \infty$ means no
atmospheric attenuation). Intersection of v and $\hat{c}$ indicates .5 probability of
detection.

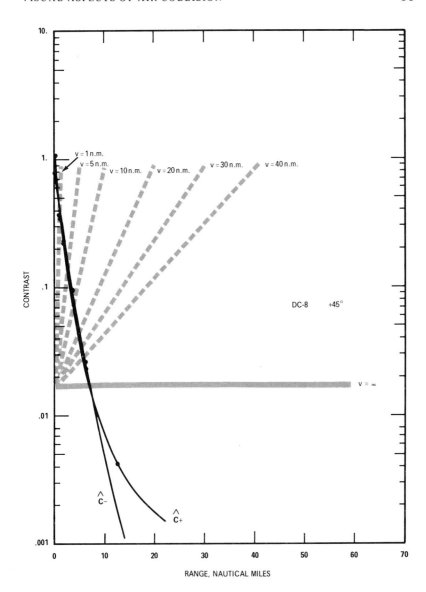

FIGURE 8   Maximum convolution contrast of DC-8 at +45° aspect as a function
of range. Maximum positive and negative contrasts are $\hat{c}$+ and $\hat{c}$-. Functions labeled v are atmospheric visibility conditions in nautical miles ($v = \infty$ means no
atmospheric attenuation). Intersection of v and $\hat{c}$ indicates .5 probability of
detection.

James L. Harris

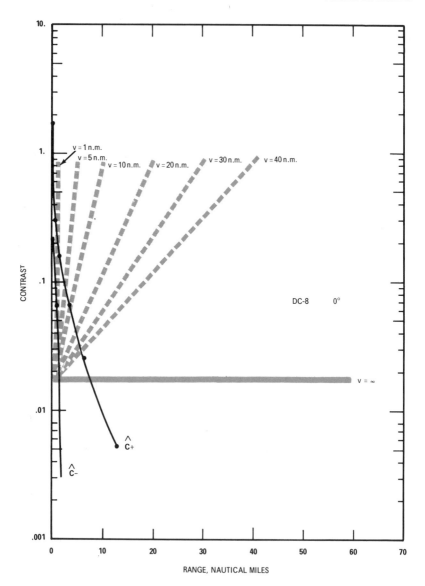

FIGURE 9   Maximum convolution contrast of DC-8 at $0°$ aspect as a function of range. Maximum positive and negative contrasts are $\hat{c}+$ and $\hat{c}-$. Functions labeled v are atmospheric visibility conditions in nautical miles ($v = \infty$ means no atmospheric attenuation). Intersection of v and $\hat{c}$ indicates .5 probability of detection.

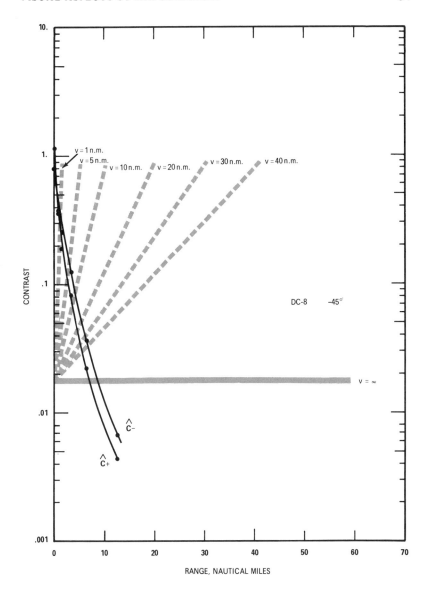

FIGURE 10 Maximum convolution contrast of DC-8 at −45° aspect as a function of range. Maximum positive and negative contrasts are $\hat{c}+$ and $\hat{c}-$. Functions labeled v are atmospheric visibility conditions in nautical miles ($v = \infty$ means no atmospheric attenuation). Intersection of v and $\hat{c}$ indicates .5 probability of detection.

38

James L. Harris

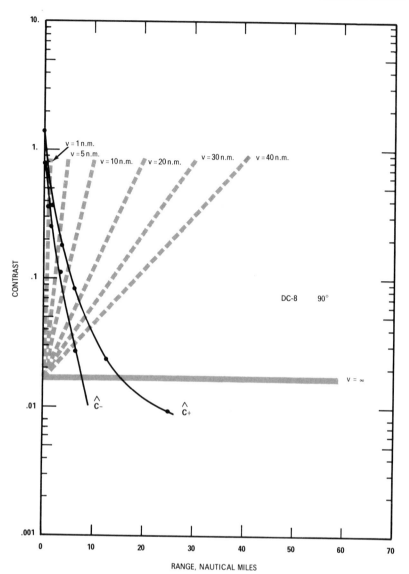

FIGURE 11   Maximum convolution contrast of DC-8 at 90° aspect as a function
of range. Maximum positive and negative contrasts are ĉ+ and ĉ−. Functions labeled v are atmospheric visibility conditions in nautical miles ($v = \infty$ means no
atmospheric attenuation). Intersection of v and $\hat{c}$ indicates .5 probability of detection.

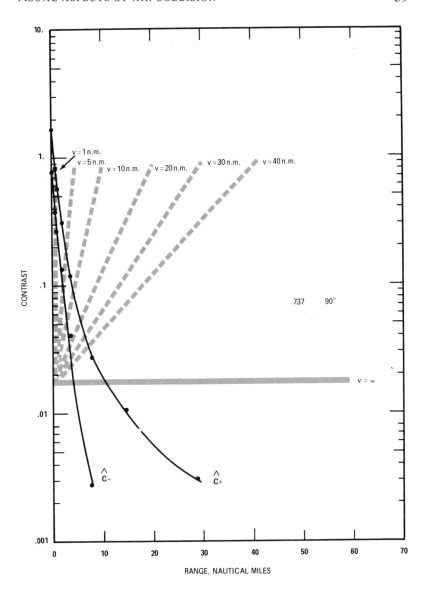

FIGURE 12 Maximum convolution contrast of 737 at 90° aspect as a function of range. Maximum positive and negative contrasts are $\hat{c}+$ and $\hat{c}-$. Functions labeled v are atmospheric visibility conditions in nautical miles ($v = \infty$ means no atmospheric attenuation). Intersection of v and $\hat{c}$ indicates .5 probability of detection.

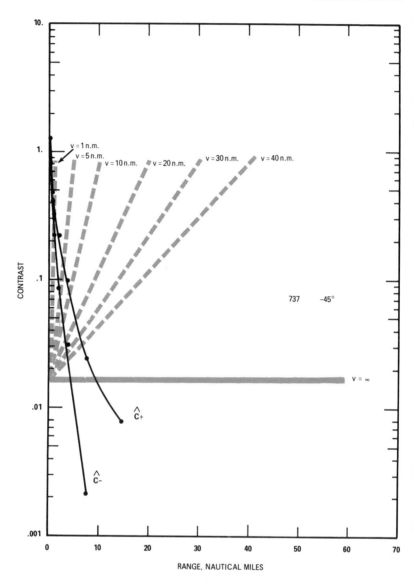

FIGURE 13 Maximum convolution contrast of 737 at $-45°$ aspect as a function of range. Maximum positive and negative contrasts are $\hat{c}+$ and $\hat{c}-$. Functions labeled v are atmospheric visibility conditions in nautical miles ($v = \infty$ means no atmospheric attenuation). Intersection of v and $\hat{c}$ indicates .5 probability of detection.

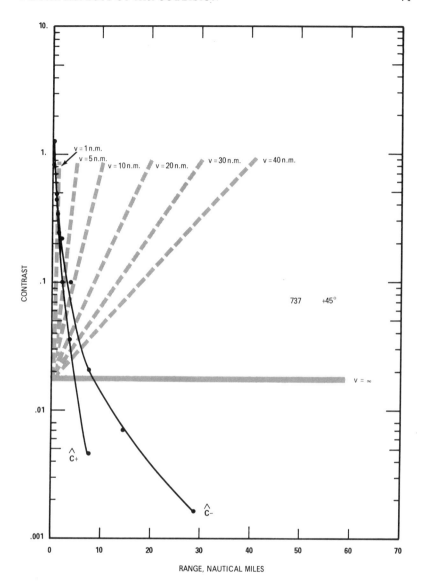

FIGURE 14 Maximum convolution contrast of 737 at +45° aspect as a function of range. Maximum positive and negative contrasts are $\hat{c}+$ and $\hat{c}-$. Functions labeled v are atmospheric visibility conditions in nautical miles ($v = \infty$ means no atmospheric attenuation). Intersection of v and $\hat{c}$ indicates .5 probability of detection.

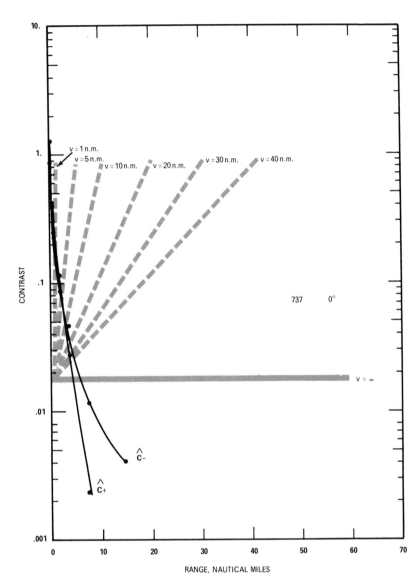

FIGURE 15   Maximum convolution contrast of 737 at $0°$ aspect as a function of range. Maximum positive and negative contrasts are $\hat{c}+$ and $\hat{c}-$. Functions labeled v are atmospheric visibility conditions in nautical miles ($v = \infty$ means no atmospheric attenuation). Intersection of v and $\hat{c}$ indicates .5 probability of detection.

can be drawn on the graph such that liminal detection range is the intersection of the convolution contrast curve and the selected meteorological range line.

While only the peak values of the convolution operation are plotted in Figures 4–15, the entire convolution map is computed. These maps have the appearance of a blurred image of the aircraft, the blur becoming more severe with increasing range. Such images are shown in Figures 16–18 for four arbitrarily selected ranges (A, B, C, D). The meaning of these images is debatable, but in a crude sense they represent a "brains-eye-view" of the aircraft. As such it is interesting to speculate that such pictures might be used to obtain quantitative

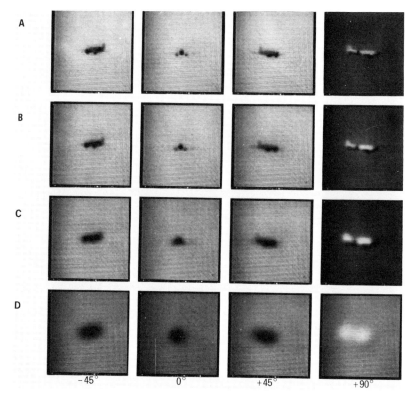

FIGURE 16 Convolution maps calculated from luminance maps shown in Figure 1(F). Rows are four arbitrarily selected ranges.

estimates of the distance at which various functions of higher order
than detection take place. For example, referring to Figure 16, at
what range can you recognize that the object is an aircraft; at what
range can you determine the aspect of the aircraft, and at what range
can you tell that it is a twin engine aircraft? The convolution pictures
also clearly show the transition with increasing range to a single contrast polarity.

Figures 4–15 show convolution contrast values for direct foveal
fixation only. For visual search, thresholds must also be determined
for peripheral vision. Figure 19 shows an extension of the calculation
for retinal image displacements with respect to the fixational center
of 0°, 2°, 4°, 6°, and 10°. Liminal threshold ranges for a single 1/3-

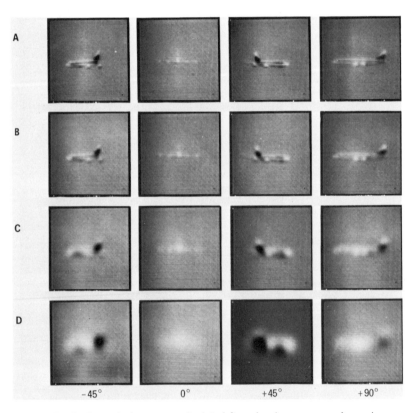

FIGURE 17   Convolution maps calculated from luminance maps shown in
Figure 3(F). Rows are four arbitrarily selected ranges.

sec fixation for each retinal position can be read from the intersection with the $\nu = \infty$ line. For example, the DC-3, +45° is detectable with direct fixation at between 10 and 11 miles, but it is
detectable at approximately 4 miles when it is 10° from the point
of fixation.

Figure 19 shows more than the range at which 50 percent threshold occurs, for it shows for all ranges the magnitude of the stimulus
relative to threshold. We refer to this as the *limen ratio*. A plot of
limen ratio is shown in Figure 20.

Limen ratio can be directly related to probability of detection
(Taylor, 1964; Blackwell, 1963). A conversion to probability is
shown in Figure 21. Here we see probability of detection for a single

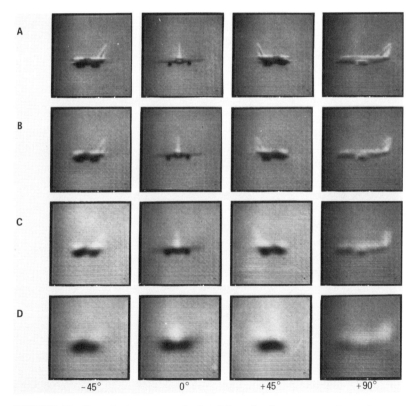

FIGURE 18   Convolution maps calculated from luminance maps shown in
Figure 2(F). Rows are four arbitrarily selected ranges.

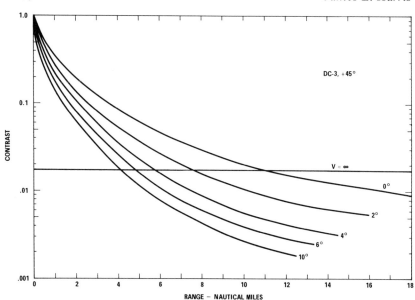

FIGURE 19 Contrast as a function of range for various amounts of eccentricity from the point of fixation ($0°$). Intersection of v with a constant function indicates .5 probability of detection (threshold).

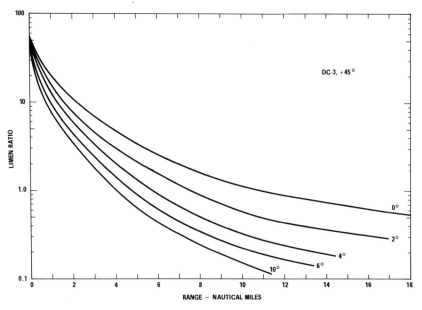

FIGURE 20 Ratio of contrast at threshold to contrast at other ranges. The contrast function for $10°$ eccentricity intersects the v function at 4 miles in Figure 19; the $10°$ function reaches unity at 4 miles in this figure.

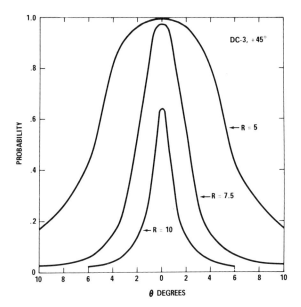

FIGURE 21   Probability of detection as a function of
eccentricity from point of fixation at various ranges.

fixation as a function of the retinal position of the aircraft image and
for selected aircraft ranges. Figure 21 corresponds to what has sometimes been called a "soft-shelled" visual detection lobe (Harris, 1959).

The complete visual detection lobe is the figure of revolution of
Figure 21. If a single fixation is made in the search field then the
volume integral of the visual detection lobe is a number whose dimension is square degrees. A plot of this integral as a function of range is
shown in Figure 22. We see that at range of 6 nautical miles the integral has a value of approximately 70 square degrees. A visual detection lobe having unity probability over a cone of 70 square degrees
and zero probability elsewhere would have an equal integral. This
may be thought of as an equivalent solid angle of coverage for each
fixation

The probability of detection for a single fixation is equal to the
equivalent solid angle of coverage divided by the total solid angle
of field to be searched. The probability per fixation is shown in
Figure 23 for an 1,800 square-degree field of search.

The final step in the calculation is to consider the dynamic situa-

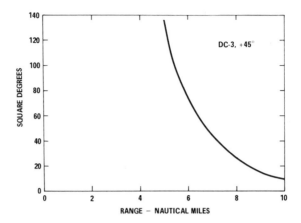

FIGURE 22 Volume integral of the detection lobes
given in Figure 21 (see text).

tion with the aircraft closing at an assumed velocity and to accumu-
late the contributions from each fixation throughout the closure.
This final step is shown in Figure 24 for an assumed closing velocity
of 360 knots. It was assumed that the fixations were located at random within the field of search.

The result shown in Figure 24 assumes that the pilot devoted full
time to the search effort. Ordinarily, cockpit duties do not allow any-
thing close to 100 percent search time. The true percentage would
certainly depend on the circumstances of the flight, which govern
cockpit workload. It would also depend heavily on the individual
flyer's habits and the relative importance that he places on visual
vigilance. A reduced percentage of time devoted to search can easily
be introduced into the calculation by returning to Figure 23, block-
ing out those range intervals where search was not being performed
and then recalculating the cumulative probability of detection to
give a new curve for Figure 24.

The material presented in this paper illustrates a technique of calculation applicable to the air collision problem. No conclusions can
be drawn from a single case involving one aircraft, one aspect, one
lighting geometry, one search solid angle, or any other single instance
of a wide variety of conditions. Similar analysis performed for a cross
section of such cases will give insight into the nature of the visual

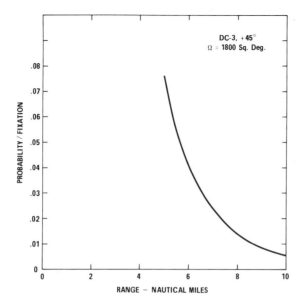

FIGURE 23   Probability of detection for a single fixation
of 1,800 square degrees as a function of range.

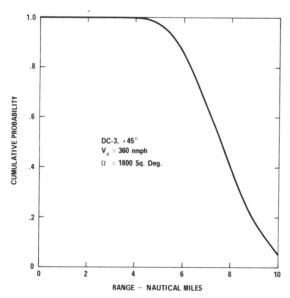

FIGURE 24   Cumulative probability of detection of an
approaching aircraft as a function of range.

capabilities in air collision avoidance. As is generally true, it is difficult
to postulate a practical solution to a problem that is not clearly under-
stood. In my opinion, the tools of analysis described in this paper can
assist in developing such an understanding. It is very easy to attribute
every air collision to "pilot error." To do so may be placing an un-
justified stigma on the pilots involved and may allow all other pilots
to continue a false optimism that it can never happen to them. A
clear understanding of the capabilities and limitations of the human
visual system in collision avoidance with full recognition of the
pilot's cockpit workload is a necessary prerequisite for the development of satisfactory solutions to the problem.

REFERENCES

Blackwell, H. R. Neural theories of simple visual discriminations. J. Opt. Soc.
    Am., 53, 129–160, 1963.
Duntley, S. Q. Visibility. Appl. Opt., 3, 550–556, 1964.
Harris, J. L. Factors to be considered in developing optimum visual search. Proc.
    Armed Forces–NRC Committee on Vision, Publication 712, 69–83, 1960.
Harris, J. L. Object classification. Appl. Opt., 3, 587–591, 1969.
Taylor, J. H. Use of visual performance data in visibility prediction. Appl. Opt.,
    3, 562–569, 1964.

HARRY L. SNYDER*
THE BOEING COMPANY

Dynamic Visual Search Patterns

Considerable research in air-to-ground acquisition of targets has found stable relationships between search performance and such variables as target characteristics (e.g., size, color, and shape), aircraft performance (speed and altitude), and environmental conditions (level and direction of illumination, visibility, and cloud cover). With these data on hand, it seemed desirable in late 1967 to attempt once again to develop a mathematical model of air-to-ground unaided visual search performance. However, in choosing to approach the problem using an integrated single-glimpse probability model, it became all too apparent that the purposive scanning patterns observed during previous experiments logically eliminated any "cookie-cutter" approach to describing the visual field. In fact, it was quite obvious that the air-to-ground observer did not search the scene in a uniform plow-share or circular pattern, as some model builders have assumed, but that the points of fixation are highly purposeful, are related to the content of the scene, may vary among observers, and certainly do not cover the total visual field. In an effort to better understand the basics of air-to-ground search behavior, then, the experiment reported here was conducted by Charles P. Greening, Richard D. Sturm, and

*Present address: Department of Industrial Engineering and Operations Research, Virginia Polytechnic Institute and State University.

Melvin J. Wyman in late 1967. It was one part of a series of air-to-ground target-acquisition experiments directed by the author for Joint Task Force Two during the period 1965–1967.

Previous experiments with air-to-ground search patterns demonstrated that performance was directly related to the type of visual scan pattern that observers were instructed to use (Thomas and Caro, 1962). Head movement directing the line of sight from the horizon abeam the aircraft inward toward the aircraft and back outward at a fixed rate (side movement method) produced significantly better identification of targets than, in descending order, the forward movement method, the forward fixed method, or the side fixed method. In the forward movement method, the observer "looked forward at a 45° angle to the line of flight initially and then swept his gaze back toward the rear of the aircraft." In the forward fixed method the observer looked at the same 45° angle to the line of flight but did not move his head. In the side fixed method, the line of sight was fixed 90° to the line of flight and downward.

The observers in the Thomas and Caro studies were not monitored for head movements during flight; rather, it was assumed that they had in fact followed their training instructions during the test flights. The consistency of the data indicate that the four groups of observers were using different patterns of search, although these patterns are much too gross for use in developing a detailed model of single-glimpse performance.

Eye-movement data obtained from other experimental situations were examined for relevance to air-to-ground search. Typically, these previous experiments have generated fixation-duration frequency distributions and relationships between time required to locate an object and fixation durations. Unfortunately, data from such tasks as radar-display search (White and Ford, 1960), symbol search (Ford *et al.*, 1959; Williams, 1967), and electronic chip inspection (Gould and Schoonard, 1969) have little applicability to the time-limited, dynamically changing air-to-ground search task.

Finally, we wished to determine how visual search might be made more efficient. Gilmour and his colleagues at Boeing have shown that for nearly all air-to-ground search conditions the observer wastes more than 40 percent of his time in useless search activity during the period after the target has become available but before an acquisition response has been made. If, during this period, many fixations are directed to irrelevant objects that are dissimilar to the target, perhaps the amount of wasted time can be reduced.

METHOD

All data were collected in the Autonetics (Anaheim, California) VFR Laboratory, which is similar to that built for Joint Task Force Two by the Sandia Corporation in Albuquerque, New Mexico, and to The Boeing Company's Multimission Simulator in Seattle.

Flight Simulation

The visual scene was projected on a spherical screen of 15-ft radius by a 70-mm motion-picture projector. The angular subtense of the projected photograph to the observer, seated in a cockpit at the screen's center of curvature, was 160° horizontal by 60° vertical. Approximately 20° of the vertical field was above the horizon in normal flight attitude. The films used in this study were aerial photographs of the Joint Task Force Two test range. The projected imagery had a limiting resolution of about 4' at a screen luminance of 20 fL. Simulated altitude was 200 ft, and simulated speed was 360 knots. Each of five subjects, all test pilots, flew two prebriefed missions, with each mission containing four targets.

Eye-Movement Recording

The eye movements were recorded from only the right eye from the time the target ceased to be obscured by the terrain until it has passed out of the field of view. Eye movements were recorded from all subjects and for all eight targets using a modified Polymetric V-0165-1 Eye-Movement Recorder. This recorder was modified by using a separate 16-mm recording camera for the visual scene (necessitated by the low luminance of the screen) and by removing the optical path beam-splitter so that the corneal reflection path was sent only to the eye-movement camera. The 16-mm scene-camera was located on one side of the headband. A spring was attached between the headband and the roof of the cockpit simulator to relieve the recorder's weight from the subject; no apparent loss in freedom of head movement resulted.

Procedure

Following a general explanation of the experiment and familiarization with the equipment, each subject was fitted with the Eye-Movement Recorder, including a bite-bar. The eye spot was then aligned to ensure that it remained in the field of view. An alignment pattern, consisting of five black squares in 11° × 11° matrix was used. This pattern was located at a distance of 13 ft from the observer's eye, with the center spot at eye level.

With all apparatus adjusted, the subject was given a familiarization flight in the simulator over a nontarget course, following which any needed adjustments in the headband, bite-bar, or other equipment were made.

The subject was then removed from the simulator and given the detailed mission briefing for the first course he was to fly. When he returned to the simulator, all of his equipment was again fitted and aligned.

Eye-Movement Recorder Alignment

Figure 1 illustrates the five-spot alignment pattern. As the subject fixated on each of the five spots, the corneal reflections associated with those spots were recorded. On projecting the eye-spot film and the test film (showing the alignment pattern upon a single, flat screen from two synchronous projectors), it is possible to adjust one of the projectors to achieve perfect alignment of the eye spots (corneal reflections) with the alignment pattern on the scene. The adjustments necessary are tilt, displacement, and scale. Tilt is correctable by rotation of either projector, while displacement is correctable by vertical and horizontal shifts in the location of either projector. Assuming a single and constant scale factor, this is most easily corrected by employing a zoom lens on either projector. Figure 1 shows a sample set of corneal reflections along with the alignment pattern.

Following alignment of the eye spot and test films for each subject and for each mission, all data were reduced by the following procedure.

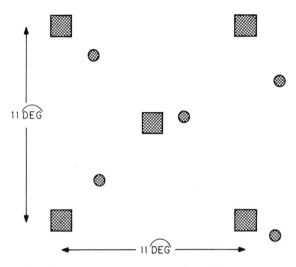

FIGURE 1   Alignment pattern used to calibrate eye-movement recorder.

Data Reduction

Films were advanced to the last frame of the final target sequence, identifiable as the last exposed frame because both cameras were turned on and off simultaneously. Any discrepancy in the total numbers of frames for the two films was noted and compensated for during data reduction. Films were then run back to the first frame and advanced frame by frame with the position of the eye spot plotted in the proper place on a series of target pictures. The target pictures were made from every fortieth frame of the 70-mm simulation film and thus represented a point every 1,100 ft in approach to the target.

The position of the point of regard was recorded for each data frame, and the duration of the fixation was measured by counting the number of data frames during which the eye spot did not move. Successive fixations were noted on the target pictures, along with the fixation at which time the subject indicated a target acquisition response by depressing a button. Fixations occurring on the assigned target were also noted. A sample of the plotting notation is given in Figure 2, omitting the target picture.

Because the 16-mm cameras were run at 14 frames per second, all fixation durations were recorded in multiples of 1/14 or 0.071 sec.

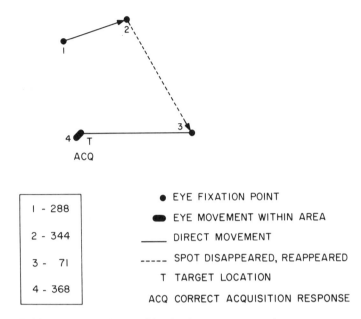

| I - 288 |
| 2 - 344 |
| 3 - 71 |
| 4 - 368 |

● EYE FIXATION POINT

⬛ EYE MOVEMENT WITHIN AREA

―― DIRECT MOVEMENT

----- SPOT DISAPPEARED, REAPPEARED

T TARGET LOCATION

ACQ CORRECT ACQUISITION RESPONSE

FIGURE 2　Notation used in plotting eye movements.

RESULTS AND DISCUSSION

Dwell-Time Distributions

The dwell-time frequency distribution for all Ss is shown in Figure 3. The median dwell-time, 320 msec, is not dissimilar from that found in other eye-movement studies; also the skewness is similar to other results. For purposes of easy comparison, the White and Ford (1960) radarscope data are overlaid. Thus, it appears that the dynamically changing stimulus scene has no significant effect upon fixation dwell-times.

In order to determine whether target acquisition performance is related to fixation dwell-time, the five observers were divided into three groups, good, medium, and poor, as shown in Table 1. The frequency distribution of dwell-times for the three groups were then plotted as shown in Figure 4.

The median dwell-times show a consistent increase as acquisition performance decreases (.288 sec, .344 sec, and .368 sec). While detailed statistical analysis is not warranted for this sample size, it is

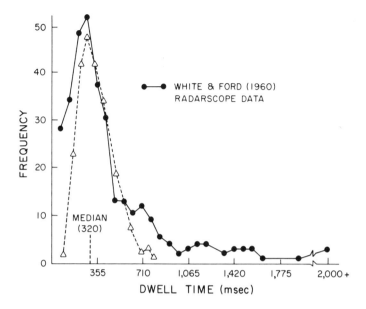

FIGURE 3   Frequency distribution of dwell-times for all subjects.

interesting to note that a median test (Siegel, 1956) showed the differences to be significant at the .06 level of confidence. This finding is consistent with the well-known reduction in dwell-times with increased reading speed (Yarbus, 1967; Woodworth and Schlosberg, 1954).

It is also interesting to note that there was no systematic variation in dwell-times as the target approached the simulated aircraft or as the subject searched closer in to the aircraft.

TABLE 1   Comparative Performance of Subjects

Ss	Percent of Target Acquisition	Range of Correct Acquisition (ft)	Group Standing
1	62	6,237	Good
2	62	5,945	Good
3	50	5,380	Medium
4	62	4,493	Poor
5	50	4,941	Poor

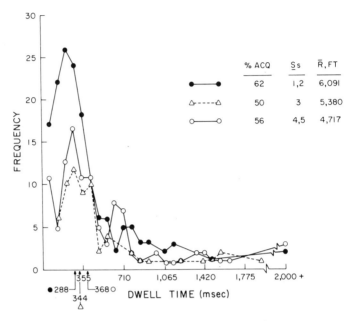

FIGURE 4   Frequency distribution of dwell-times for subjects classified by their detection performance (see text and Table 1).

Search Pattern*

It might be hypothesized, based on search patterns found in earlier studies (Ford *et al.*, 1959; White and Ford, 1960), that the fixations would sweep out much of the entire scene either randomly or systematically. Data such as these have led many theorists to assume such a plow-share or pushbroom pattern in their models so that they could achieve greater mathematical simplicity. The records of this study, however, do not reveal such a pattern. The fixations were heavily concentrated near the horizon in the center of the field. In addition, they tended to occur in certain types of terrain (e.g., clearings, roads) rather than in random or geometric patterns.

Figures 5 and 6 illustrate the recorded fixation points for all subjects on the four East Course targets and the four West Course tar-

---

*At this point, the audience at the meeting was shown a sequence of color target slides with the search patterns overlaid. Unfortunately, reproduction for this volume was not possible.

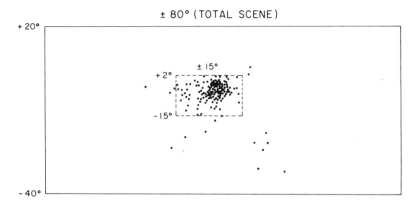

FIGURE 5   Loci of fixation points on East Course.

gets, respectively. It can be seen that 80–90 percent of the fixations fall within about 5 percent of the visual scene.

Figures 7 and 8 show the target locations for all targets for each reproduced frame of data. It is apparent that the targets generally lay in the same area as the fixations.

Target Characteristics

It was stated above that search patterns seemed to be related to target and terrain characteristics, not to any geometric or random pattern.

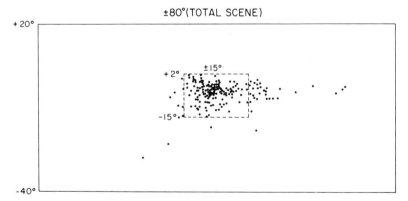

FIGURE 6   Loci of fixation points on West Course.

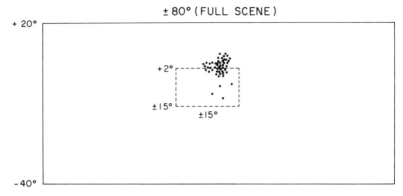

FIGURE 7   Loci of target locations on East Course (includes all frames from which data were recorded).

This hypothesis was checked by reference to the debriefing records, in which each *S* was asked to indicate which characteristic(s) of each target he used to acquire the target. Responses to this question were then checked against eye-movement records. The results, shown in Table 2, illustrate that nearly three fourths of all fixations were on features closely resembling the terrain features reported.

The wide use of road patterns or other man-made grids as references corroborates the results of LaPorte and Calhoun (1966), who

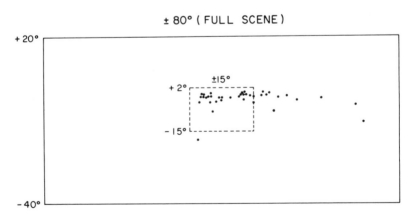

FIGURE 8   Loci of target locations on West Course (includes all frames from which data were recorded).

TABLE 2 Correlation of Fixations with Reported Terrain Cues

Stated Characteristics	Fixations on Characteristics (n)	Total Fixations (N)	n/N
Units in clearing	17	22	0.77
Field pattern	9	18	0.50
Road pattern	23	26	0.88
Field and road pattern	20	32	0.62
Truck park pattern	21	25	0.84
Highway	17	20	0.85
Town and runway	7	13	0.54
Town and warehouse	20	26	0.77
River, road, bridge structure	21	34	0.62
River bend	23	29	0.79
	245	178	0.73

did not measure eye movements but did use verbal reports on types of cues used in target search. Both studies are consistent with a cognitive approach to target acquisition, as opposed to a simple pattern-matching scheme. The briefing material indicates that the S tends to estimate those characteristics of target *and background* that will be most apparent at a distance, and then searches for those. He uses the detailed appearance of the target itself more as a check in positive identification.

Several times during this experiment, the observer located the target area, fixated it, and still did not make an acquisition response. The eye-movement records indicate when this happened but offer no explanation of the failure to respond. Clearly, any predictive search model must take account of such presently unexplainable events.

Quality of the Data

Collecting this type of data is difficult for several reasons. The wide-angle (160°) search situation requires free head movement of the S while, at the same time, fixation points are being accurately recorded. The helmet-mounted camera and light assembly, while fairly rigidly fixed with bite-bar, chin strap, and headband, is not perfectly fixed to the head; consequently, movements of a few thousandths of an inch can occur. During such movements and during blinks, the corneal reflection is lost and measurements cannot be made. Equipment failures also occurred. In sum, the total number of completely usable records from the five subject searching for eight targets was 15, instead of the possible 40. It is believed that the 15 records obtained are free of major calibration errors. It is estimated that the fixation errors were within $\pm 2°$, or about 1/8 in. on the 8 X 10 in. target pictures.

CONCLUSIONS

The data obtained in this study, although exploratory in nature, permit the following conclusions:

1. The search process is largely cognitive and involves detailed visual pattern-matching only as a final verification of target identity;

2. The characteristics of the surrounding terrain and its associated cultural features are at least as important as the characteristics of the target itself;

3. Superior target acquisition performance is associated with shorter dwell-times;

4. The search behavior exhibited here is inadequate for detecting off-flight-path targets due to the restricted angular area in which fixations occurred;

5. With regard to development of a mathematical model of visual search, the following implications should be noted: First, fixation durations of .3 to .4 sec are approximately invariant with target type, target range, and likelihood of acquisition; second, the probability that a fixation will fall on any particular portion of the image is highly dependent on the resemblance of that portion to the expected appearance of the target or target cues; third, the probability of looking at a target falls off very rapidly as the target departs from the ground track or velocity vector of the aircraft;

6. Training techniques that reduce dwell-times are likely to increase the range of target acquisition. Some operational advantages might be obtained for the military in this manner.

REFERENCES

Ford, A., C. T. White, and M. Lichtenstein. Analysis of eye movements during free search. J. Opt. Soc. Am., 49, 287–292, 1959.

Gould, J. D., and J. W. Schoonard. Eye Movements during Visual Inspection of Integrated Circuit Chips. IBM Research Center, 1969.

LaPorte, H. R., and R. L. Calhoun, Laboratory Studies in Air-to-Ground Target Recognition: X. Clue Utilization in Target Recognition. Autonetics Report T6-1504/3111, July 1966.

Siegel, S. Nonparametric Statistics for Behavioral Sciences. McGraw-Hill, New York, 1956.

Thomas, F. H., and P. W. Caro, Jr. Training Research on Low Altitude Visual Aerial Observation: A Description of Five Field Experiments. HumRRO Research Memorandum 8, July 1962.

White, C. T., and A. Ford. Eye movements during simulated radar search. J. Opt. Soc. Am., 50, 909–913, 1960.

Williams, L. G. A Study of Visual Search Using Eye Movement Recordings. Minneapolis-Honeywell Document 12009-IR3, March 1967.

Woodworth, R. S., and H. Schlosberg. Experimental Psychology. Holt and Co., New York, 1954.

Yarbus, A. L. Eye Movements and Vision. Plenum Press, New York, 1967.

HERSCHEL W. LEIBOWITZ
THE PENNSYLVANIA STATE UNIVERSITY

Detection of Peripheral Stimuli under Psychological and Physiological Stress

The impetus for the present paper stems in part from the 1959 annual meeting of the Committee on Vision, which was also devoted to visual search. During that meeting, Fry (1960) stressed the point that peripheral vision plays an important role in triggering subsequent eye movements. Although peripheral vision is degraded as a result of the coarseness of the retinal mosaic and optical aberrations, the available cues are significant in determining where the eye will look next. As an illustration, one could imagine how difficult it would be to attempt to scan the entire visual field with the fovea. Clearly, the magnitude of eye movements and the time required to make them would greatly decrease the efficiency of the search process. To accomplish a search task in a reasonable period of time, one must make use of peripheral vision. Empirical evidence supporting this assumption is provided by Smith (1961) and Erickson (1964), who demonstrated that visual search capability is correlated with peripheral discrimination.

There is no question that the periphery, which encompasses most of the visual field, is important when considering the functional per-

*This research was supported by grant ME 08061 from the National Institutes of Health, contract CPE-69-110 from the Environmental Control Administration, HEW, USPHS, and the Transportation Research Center, Pennsylvania State University.

64

formance of the eye, but a primary concern in this presentation is
that the contribution of peripherally presented stimuli is variable.
An interesting example of this can be found in Burg's data (1968a)
on the extent of the nasal-lateral visual field (Figure 1). These measurements were obtained as part of a large-scale study in which a
battery of visual tests was given to thousands of subjects in an attempt to determine which visual functions correlate with subsequent
automobile accidents. The area of the nasal field, obtained from more
than 17,000 subjects, increases with age up to a maximum between
30 and 40 years, followed by a progressive decline. The decrease in
field size with age might be explained by the increasing opacity of
the ocular media or diminution in the size of the pupil. However,
the increase cannot be explained by the same mechanism, so one
could hypothesize that the subjects in this age group were somehow
learning to make more efficient use of their peripheral vision. Similarly, there is no obvious physiological explanation for the superiority
of the females. It has been suggested that while it is polite for males
in our society to look directly at females, the converse is considered
bad taste. Therefore, females learn to use peripheral vision as part of

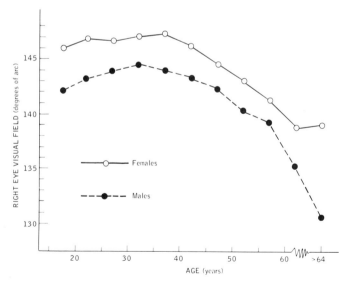

FIGURE 1   Angular extent of visual field of the right eye as a function of age; after Burg (1968).

their normal adjustment pattern to our social mores. Although this suggestion was originally made partially in jest, in involves the principle, which I feel has some merit, that the use of peripheral vision is not determined solely by physiological factors but, rather, that learning and experience play an important role.

A large number of studies illustrate the principle that the effect of peripherally presented stimuli is variable. A generalization emerging from these data is that when foveally and peripherally presented stimuli compete for attention, the peripheral stimuli have lower priority. I mention Burg's data because of the large number of subjects tested and because his significant research program was reported to a previous meeting of the Committee on Vision (1968b). However, the data on which these generalizations are based involve a variety of experiments from many laboratories utilizing different experimental variables and procedures. Gasson and Peters (1965) found significant shrinkage in the size of the visual field as measured perimetrically when concentrating on a demanding foveal task. Similarly, Bursill (1958) reports a decrease in the accuracy of detection of peripheral signals under adverse thermal conditions when the perceptual load of a central tracking task was high. Bahrick *et al.* (1952) demonstrated that when they improved performance on a tracking task with incentives, detection of peripheral stimuli worsened. Webster and Haslerud (1964) found decreased peripheral performance when the subject was asked to count flashes or auditory clicks. The influence of danger-induced stress was illustrated by Weltman and Egstrom (1966) in a study that showed that novice divers attend less well to peripheral stimuli in a stressful situation. Kobrick and Dusek (1970) found an increase in peripheral reaction time as a result of hypoxia.

The principle that the efficacy of peripheral vision can vary widely is reflected in a number of concepts. Sanders (1966), in summarizing the results of a series of experiments on information processing, refers to the functional or effective visual field, which shrinks or expands depending on the perceptual load of the task. Mackworth (1965) alludes to a similar process in stating that visual noise causes functional tunnel vision. A similar notion is inherent in the theorizing of the developmental psychology of Piaget (Vurpillot, 1959). His notions of *centration* and *decentration* are similar, at a more cognitive level, to those of Sanders and Mackworth. Easterbrook (1959) discusses the "range of cue utilization" and concludes that the number of cues utilized in any situation becomes smaller with increase in motion. In clinical neurology, the phenomenon of "sparing the macula" represents an analogous process.

Indeed, in looking over this literature, I am impressed with the number and variety of studies demonstrating variability in the utilization of peripherally presented information. Whereas information presented to the fovea has a very high probability of being effective, the corresponding effectiveness of peripherally presented stimuli depends upon both the nature of the task and the condition of the observer. It is interesting to note that this principle, presented here as an abstraction from the experimental literature, is accepted as a working hypothesis by athletic coaches. They assume, on an entirely different basis, that good peripheral vision is essential to superior performance in perceptual motor skills (McVay, 1968).

We have investigated this problem in our own laboratory by determining luminance thresholds in the presence of a competing foveal task (Leibowitz and Appelle, 1969). The experimental arrangement was a perimeter with a central fixation light and 12 peripheral stimuli each subtending 1.07° mounted from 20° to 90° in the horizontal plane on both sides of the fixation point. The subject was instructed to maintain fixation and to indicate when a light appeared in the periphery. Observation was binocular in total darkness. The functions obtained in the conventional manner, with a steady fixation light, are given by the solid line in Figure 2. The absolute threshold is minimal at 20° of eccentricity and increases steadily as more and more peripheral areas are stimulated. These data are very similar to those obtained by Sloan (Chapanis, 1949). In order to introduce competition for attention, the fixation light was interrupted, and the subject had to press a button to relight it. Thus, in the control condition, the only task was to report the presence of a light in the periphery, while the experimental condition involved the additional task of responding to extinction of the fixation light. Data were obtained for two interruption rates of the fixation light, as indicated in Figure 2. It should be noted that with the additional central task, the peripheral thresholds were increased for both interruption rates. The increase is mostly in the near periphery and amounts to between one third and one log

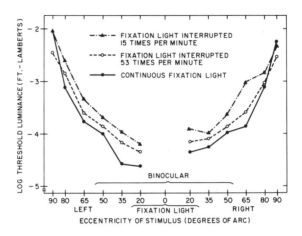

FIGURE 2   Log mean luminance threshold as a function of stimulus eccentricity. For the control group, fixation was maintained on a steady light. For the experimental groups, the subjects were required to maintain illumination of the interrupted fixation light by pressing a button.

unit. Beyond 65° of eccentricity, the additional task has little effect.

    When we planned this experiment, we did not consider the possibility that learning would improve the discrimination of peripherally presented stimuli. This may have been partly due to my training in classical sensory physiology, which usually ignored such factors. However, we did note that the experimental groups in the threshold experiment tended to improve over the three testing sessions. In order to determine the specific influence of learning, Abernethy (1968) carried out a study using the same apparatus and procedure but gave the subject feedback after each peripheral light was presented. Specifically, if a subject missed a light, he was so informed and the light was reilluminated at a higher level so that he would notice it. In order to analyze the effect of learning, the plots of these data for the five sessions are presented in Figure 3. It can be seen that the results of the final session were similar to the results obtained both by Sloan (Chapanis, 1949) and by our previous experiment (Leibowitz and Appelle, 1969). The initial session is approximately two log units higher than the final session for practice produces progressively lower thresholds, which approach some limit.

In both of these experiments, we were interested in observing the level of performance with respect to the fixation light. As a reflection of the generalization stated previously that priority is given to the central task, no changes in the performance of this task were found; more specifically, neither study showed a difference in mean reaction time for the central task in the two interruption rates used. Further, increasing experience produced no changes in performance of the central task in Abernethy's study.

It is clear from these experiments that the ability to detect peripheral stimuli is influenced by a simultaneously presented central task. For the inexperienced subjects in Abernethy's experiment, this impairment amounts to two log units, a value that is highly significant in vision research. Furthermore, these differences are not necessarily permanent. If one assumes that the problem is one of spreading attention over a wider visual field, then the learning data must be interpreted in terms of the ability of the subject to improve or acquire this ability with experience.

As usually happens in the laboratory when new measures are being investigated, the two experiments I have just described had an influence on other studies. Olsen (1970), who is interested in the effects

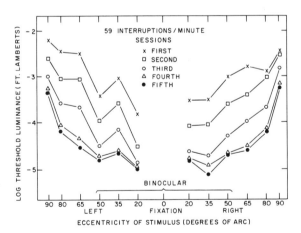

FIGURE 3   Log mean luminance threshold as a function of stimulus eccentricity for five sessions. The subjects were required to maintain illumination of the fixation light that was interrupted 59 times per minute.

of fatigue on the performance of automobile drivers, introduced a peripheral vision task into a driving simulator. The subjects were required to move a steering wheel to track a spot of light while at the same time reporting on the presence of peripheral stimuli. In one phase of his study, subjects were tested continuously in marathon sessions lasting from 6½ to 9½ hr without a break. Under these severe conditions, the performance of both the tracking and the peripheral tasks deteriorated. Furthermore, performance was cyclical; it would worsen and then improve again. Although performance and the central and peripheral tasks were correlated to some extent, the relative degradation of performance on the peripheral task was worse than for the central task. A summary of Olsen's data, representing the maximum, minimum, and median reaction-time values throughout the marathon sessions, is reproduced in Figure 4. The closeness of the minimum and median reaction times suggests that the subjects performed remarkably well most of the time. There were, however,

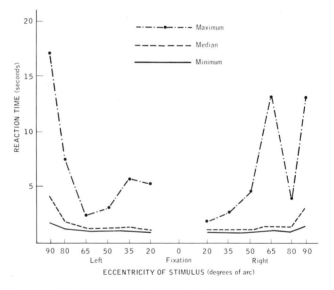

FIGURE 4   Maximum, median, and minimum reaction times to peripherally located stimuli during long sessions in a driving simulator. The subjects were simultaneously engaged in a pursuit tracking task. The sessions for the five subjects lasted between 6½ and 9½ hr without interruption; after Olsen (1970).

periods of markedly inferior performance with corresponding implications for the efficiency of the driver. Unfortunately, it is not possible to give a complete analysis of Olsen's data except to point out that they agree with and, in fact, contribute to the generalizations stated so far regarding central and peripheral stimulation.

At this point, Bar-Or, Hennessy, Abernethy, and I were fortunate in being asked to participate in a study carried out at the Human Performance Laboratory at Penn State on the influence of dehydration on performance. The purpose of this experiment was to analyze the effect of heat stress and the resulting dehydration. Subjects were to spend 8 hr in an environmental test chamber maintained at 105°F. In a single daily session two subjects would alternate in walking on a treadmill for 20 min throughout a 6-hr period. The speed and inclination of the treadmill were adjusted so as to produce a predetermined weight loss of either 2.5 percent or 5 percent in 6 hr.

It will be recognized that loss of 5 percent of body weight reflects considerable heat stress. For an overweight person, however, the physiological effects of fluid loss are even greater. This is because the water is lost from the nonfat body mass. Since the percentage is based on the total weight, the actual fluid loss for an obese person increases in proportion to his excess weight.

These experiments were carried out under strict medical supervision. The subjects were carefully screened on the basis of physical examinations. Rectal temperature and electrocardiogram were continuously monitored throughout the study by a physician.

A large number of physiological tests were made in the course of the study. [For details, see Dukes-Dobos (1970).] We welcomed this invitation as an excellent opportunity to obtain data on visual behavior in an actual stress situation. We acted on what we had learned in previous studies of peripheral vision and we installed a perimeter of lights in the environmental chamber. The subject, while walking on the treadmill, observed foveally a circle of lights, one of which was illuminated approximately six times per min. One of the peripheral lights was illuminated approximately every 40 sec. The subject indicated by a double throw hand-held switch whenever a light appeared either centrally or peripherally. Data were obtained during the first and last 5 min of every other 20-min walking period. There were eight subjects, four whom were male, four female; four were

obese, four thin. Each subject was tested for four sessions at the two
levels of weight loss, with and without replacement of body fluids.
Results of this experimentation, which produced more than 7,000
reaction-time measurements, were, in the words of William James,
"just nothing." We found no change whatsoever in peripheral or
central reaction-time as a function of dehydration, obesity, time in
the chamber, or any of the other experimental variables. Although
the stress described so far is considerable, we were given an opportunity to test under even more severe conditions.

I indicated that the data were obtained while the subjects were
on the treadmill during the first 6 hr of an 8-hr session. The last 2
hr were set aside for physiological tests in the heat chamber. Partway
through the experiment the physiologists introduced a new measurement, known in work physiology as a "maximum performance test."
In this procedure, the inclination and speed of the treadmill are increased systematically, with the object of driving the heart rate to its
maximum. As the workload is increased, the subject is literally forced
to run to keep up with the treadmill. The heart rate increases exponentially and finally reaches an asymptote beyond which it simply
will not beat any faster. This rate is approximately 200 beats per
minute for a young adult. One significance of this test is that the
maximum heart rate cannot be maintained for a very long period
of time. As the test is continued, the blood supplied to the heart
muscle itself is threatened, and, in order to maintain it, blood is
withdrawn from the legs and head with the result that the subject
will soon collapse. The objective of the maximum performance test
is to push the subject just to the point of collapse in order to determine the maximum heart rate. These maximum tests were performed
at the end of the testing day after the subjects had been in the hot
room for 8 hr, had spent 3 hr on the treadmill, and suffered as much
as 5 percent weight loss. We welcomed the opportunity to obtain peripheral reaction time data during the maximum performance test
since this represented, as far as we know, the most severe stress that
one could produce experimentally under conditions that permit simultaneous visual experimentation.

The results, however, were again completely negative. The reaction
times to both the central and peripheral stimuli obtained during the
approximately 2 to 3 min of the performance test were the same as

those in the previous phases of the experiment. Thus, even under a condition of stress that was specifically designed to bring the subjects to the point of physiological collapse, there was no impairment in their ability to detect either central or peripherally presented stimuli (Figure 5).

At first glance, it might appear that these data on the effects of heat stress disagree with those cited previously. In the Abernethy study, even though the initial thresholds were as high as 100 times the standard values, this discrepancy disappeared after a few sessions of feedback training. In the heat study, because of the necessary physiological monitoring, practice sessions were given to all the subjects before the testing began. Since by its very nature, the stress resulting from dehydration increases slowly, the stress was introduced gradually, so that the subjects had an opportunity to practice peripheral discriminations even during an actual testing section. Considering the maximum performance test, this was administered after the subjects had a preliminary experience with the apparatus and

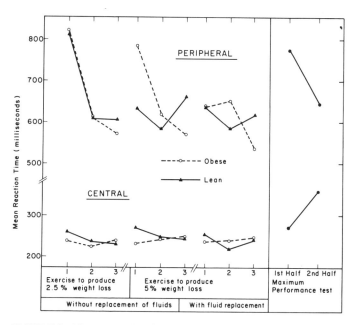

FIGURE 5 Mean central and peripheral reaction-times as a function of sessions for the various conditions of the experiment.

after several complete sessions, each of which involved a total of 45 min experience with the peripheral task. It should be noted that walking on a treadmill is extremely boring. The subject is required to move at an externally induced rate for 20 min in an uncomfortable environment that is made even more unpleasant by the attachment of physiological monitoring equipment, so the addition of the peripheral task was a welcomed respite from the unpleasant monotony of the main experiment. The subjects knew that the visual test would be of short duration and apparently were able to achieve and maintain their normal performance levels for these short time-periods. Although the failure to find any differences during the maximum performance test was a surprise to us, these data are understandable in terms of the ability of the subjects under proper conditions of motivation and experience to perform a peripheral detection task under extremely difficult conditions. The difference between the heat–stress experiment and Olsen's marathon drivers should be noted. Although optimum performance can be maintained by motivated experienced subjects for short time-periods, these results should not be generalized to a vigilance task.

To summarize the results of these experiments, I suggest that a distinction between the functional and the physiological visual fields is significant in evaluating the performance of the organism in any situation involving peripherally presented information. A large number of conditions that do not exist in the normal laboratory environment may diminish the ability to process peripherally presented information. However, this diminution can, to some extent, be eliminated by training. The generality of these relations is of course limited to the range of conditions used in the previously described experiments. Although we have pushed cardiovascular stress as far as one can reasonably hope, we have not introduced variables such as perceptual-motor load or emotional stress over very wide ranges. Whether it is possible to maintain peripheral discrimination in extreme degrees of various kinds of stress, or combinations thereof, is a question that can only be answered by experiment. Certainly, the data for the marathon driving experiments suggest that peripheral discrimination is impaired in severe vigilance tasks. In any event, the data so far indicate clearly that the contribution of the peripheral visual field is variable and must be considered in order to understand the functional performance of the visual system. At the 1965 annual meeting of the Committee on Vision, Jampolsky (1965), in summarizing the presented papers, stated

the point was made that the measured eye is not necessarily the operating or functioning eye. The functional employment of the visual capability is worthy of consideration, and development of devices for such determination is challenging and appropriate. Unique tests requiring other than the usual and traditional measurement techniques will be necessary to get at the knotty problem of perception, and the perceptual mass developed through experience, in order to assess adequately the visual capabilities of detection, tracking, etc.

I would suggest that the contribution of peripherally presented information is a measure which admirably fits these requirements.

REFERENCES

Abernethy, C. N. The Effect of Feedback on Luminance Thresholds for Peripherally Presented Stimuli under Two Conditions of Average Task Frequency. Master's Thesis, The Pennsylvania State University, 1968.

Bahrick, H. P., P. M. Fitts, and R. E. Rankin. Effect of incentives upon reactions to peripheral stimuli. J. Exp. Psych., 44, 400–406, 1952.

Bursill, A. E. Restriction of peripheral vision during exposure to hot and humid conditions. Q. J. Exp. Psych., 10, 113–129, 1958.

Burg, A. Lateral visual field as related to age and sex. J. Appl. Psych., 52(1), 10–15, 1968a.

Burg, A. Vision and driving. In Current Developments in Optics and Vision, W. Benson and M. A. Whitcomb, eds. Armed Forces–NRC Committee on Vision, NAS–NRC, 1968b.

Chapanis, A. How We See: A Summary of Basic Principles. In Human factors in undersea warfare. Panel on Psychology to Physiology, Committee on Undersea Warfare, National Research Council, Washington, D.C., 1949.

Dukes-Dobos, F. M., E. R. Buskirk, O. Bar-Or, and A. Henschel. Effect of dehydration on tolerance to exercise in heat as influenced by acclimation, obesity, and sex. Physiologist, 13, 184, 1970.

Easterbrook, J. A. The effect of emotion on cue utilization and the organization of behavior. Psych. Rev., 66, 183–201, 1959.

Erickson, R. A. Relation between visual search time and peripheral visual acuity. Hum. Factors, 165–177, 1964.

Fry, G. A. Quoted in Visual Search Techniques, A. Morris and E. P. Horne, eds., Armed Forces–NRC Committee on Vision, NAS–NRC, Washington, D.C., 233, 1960.

Gasson, A. P., and G. S. Peters. The effect of concentration upon the apparent size of the visual field in binocular vision. Optician, Part I, 148, 660–665; Part II, 149, 5–12, 1965.

Kobrick, J. L., and E. R. Dusek. Effects of hypoxia on voluntary response time to peripherally located visual stimuli. J. Appl. Phys., 29, 444–448, 1970.

Jampolsky, A. Quoted in The Measurement of Visual Function, Whitcomb, M.A., ed., Armed Forces–NRC Committee on Vision, NAS–NRC, Washington, D.C., 259, 1965.

Leibowitz, H. W., and S. Appelle. The effect of a central task on luminance thresholds for peripherally presented stimuli. Hum. Factors, 11(4), 387–392, 1969.

Mackworth, N. H. Visual noise causes tunnel vision. Psychonomic Sci. 3, 67–68, 1965.

McVay, I. R. U.S.C.'s jet-speed powerhouse. Look, 117, October 15, 1968.

Olsen, R. A. Detection of Events in the Visual Periphery during Pursuit Tracking in Long-term Performance and in Hypnotically Induced Fatigue. Ph.D. Dissertation, The Pennsylvania State University, 1970.

Sanders, A. F. Peripheral viewing and cognitive organization. In Studies in Perception, Institute for Perception, Soesterberg, Netherlands, 1966.

Smith, S. W. Visual search time and peripheral discriminability. J. Opt. Soc. Am., 51, 1462a, 1961.

Vurpillot, E. Piaget's law of relative centrations. Acta Psychol., 16, 403–430, 1959.

Webster, R. G., and G. M. Haslerud. Influence on extreme peripheral vision of attention to a visual or auditory task. J. Exp. Psych., 68, 269–272, 1964.

Weltman, G., and G. H. Egstrom. Perceptual narrowing in novice divers. Hum. Factors, 8, 499–506, 1966.

LEON G. WILLIAMS
HONEYWELL, INC.

Studies of Extrafoveal Discrimination and Detection

For several years, my colleagues and I have been studying how subjects search for targets in visual fields. I shall tell you about our point of view and about some of the experiments we have conducted. Our objective has been to predict visual search performance (measured as the probability of finding the target over the course of time) for a given set of conditions. We try to answer questions such as: How does size, color, or shape of the target affect performance? Which background characteristics affect performance or, in general, what measurable characteristics of the visual field can be used to predict performance? We have been concerned with such tasks as the search for a ship at sea, the detection of an aircraft, the search for a man, the search for a symbol on a map or a wall display, or simply the search for a circle amid other circles. The subject searches for a target about which something (but not everything) is known, and the target usually cannot be found immediately.

I shall now describe our frame of reference. Overtly, search consists of a sequence of visual fixations eventually stopping at the target. Our problem then becomes the prediction of things about

*This work has been supported by the Engineering Psychology Branch, Office of Naval Research, under Contract NONR 4774 (00) and by the Aerospace Medical Research Laboratories at Wright-Patterson AFB under Contract No. AF33(615)-3558.

the sequence—where the fixations will fall and how many there will be. Search and the fixation sequence depends on two processes: (a) an extrafoveal process, whereby objects are acquired, and (b) a foveal process, whereby objects are identified or classified. We have been concerned mainly with extrafoveal acquisition, so the targets in our experiments have been relatively easy to identify. Figure 1 illustrates the general search process.

Because we find it useful to distinguish between two kinds of acquisition, we see two kinds of search tasks, two models of the search process, and two experimental paradigms. In the first type of acquisition, targets are superthreshold extrafoveally. By this I mean that an object several degrees away from the subject's line of sight is recognizable as a potential target (that is, a member of the target class). In the second type of acquisition, the target is at threshold extrafoveally because it is small, its contrast is low, or it is embedded in the background structure. In the present discussion we shall consider only superthreshold targets. An example of this type of situation is shown in Figure 2. Here, the subject searches for a target defined either by its size, color, shape, or various combinations of these characteristics. The target is identified by a two-digit number. In this type of situation, a subject's fixations usually fall on objects. He fixates one object after another until he comes to the target. Efficient performance occurs when the subjects fixates only those objects in the specified target class (for example, it is the same size or color as the specified target). Performance depends on extrafoveal discriminability of the target from other objects, the subject's fixation rate, and identification difficulties that affect fixation rate.

A key point in our analysis is that we measure the extrafoveal discrimination between objects by observing the fixations on those objects. More specifically, we define the discriminability of a given class of objects from the specified target class by what we call the *relative fixation rate*. This is determined by the number of fixations on the given class of objects relative to the number on the specified target class. For example, when searching for a target specified as blue, the number of fixations on orange objects divided by the number on blue objects defines the relative fixation rate. When this ratio is low, it is taken to mean that blue objects are well discriminated from orange ones. Sometimes we use the term "similarity" rather than

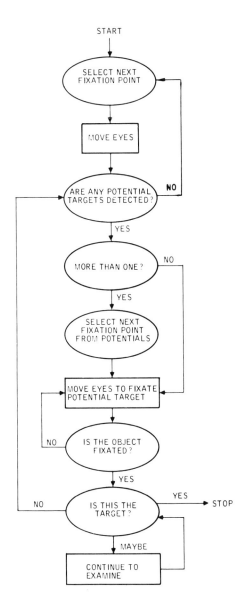

FIGURE 1   The general search process.

FIGURE 2   A search field–Study 1.

"discriminability." Thus, a high relative fixation rate implies high similarity between classes of objects. Although the relative fixation rate is usually less than unity, it can be higher. One might fixate orange objects more often than blue when searching for a blue target. Relative fixation rate is a way of scaling extrafoveal discriminability or similarity that we have found reliable and useful. In our experiments, we have measured similarity, so defined, for a range of situations. It then becomes a relatively simple matter to predict the search time, once we know the similarity of each object in the field to the target. Median search time for a given task can be predicted from the equation below (Williams, 1967):

$$t_{\mathrm{MED}} = \frac{\Sigma\, Si}{2R} + D \equiv \frac{\Sigma\, Si}{6} + \tfrac{1}{2},$$

where the summation includes all of the objects in the field, R is the mean number of objects fixated per second (typically about three per second), and D is a delay resulting from response or identification time (about .5 sec for easily identified targets).

EXPERIMENTATION

General Method

In our experiments we set up a search task, one target among many objects in the field, and we measure discriminability by determining which objects the subject fixates during search. Very briefly, I shall describe some of the experimental details.

The search fields were square, ranging from 30 to 40 degrees of visual angle (dva) in width viewed from 3 to 7 ft. There would always be a single target among 40 to 100 other objects, each typically about 1.0 dva. Some target characteristics were specified. Since there were several other objects in the field having the same characteristics, the target could only be uniquely identified by an alphanumeric label or other means. This identification was designed to be visible foveally but not extrafoveally. The targets in all studies except the first were defined by example. Thus, when searching for a target of given size, an object of that size would be displayed for reference. The trial was ended after some predetermined time, usually 30 sec.

In each study 20 to 30 subjects searched for up to 100 trials for one or more sessions. The data from about one third of the trials would be discarded because of various malfunctions in the apparatus.

The main experimental data were the eye-fixation records from which we determined each object that the subject fixated during each trial. The latest version of our apparatus is shown in Figure 3. We used the corneal reflection technique: A near-infrared source reflected from the cornea creates a virtual image, which is photographed. The position of this virtual image corresponds closely to the subject's point of fixation. We photograph it with a camera fitted with a long-focus lens. Since subjects typically fixate about three points each second,

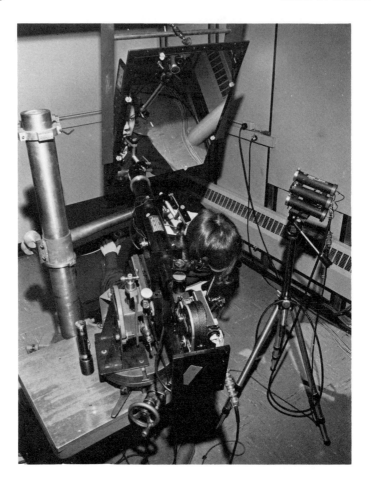

FIGURE 3   Apparatus for recording eye fixations.

it is convenient to use a series of 4-sec-long time-exposures during
each trial. The clusters of fixations on each frame projected on a representation of the search field can then be used to identify the fixated
objects. During scoring we also used a square 7 X 7 calibration matrix.
A long time-exposure of a subject's fixations as he scans the matrix, as
shown in Figure 4, is an important aid in our scoring process.

The preceding paragraphs describe all of the following studies. The
results are based on 50,000 to 100,000 scored fixations for each study.
Studies 1–4 are described in detail in Williams (1966, 1967).

Study 1—Multidimensional Target Specifications

The main purpose was to study subjects' fixations to determine if our framework was consistent with their behavior.

Objects differed in size, color, and shape. Within each object was a two-digit number. The target was specified by some or all of its characteristics and also by its two-digit identifier. Thus, the target might be described as "LARGE, RED, SQUARE—23" or simply "BLUE—47." Figure 2 is an example.

We found that subjects did tend to fixate objects having the specified characteristics. For the range of variations that we used, color was a much more potent variable than size and shape. Size, perhaps, was slightly better than shape. One interesting finding was that when two or more target characteristics were specified, subjects tended to ignore the less potent characteristic. The data are summarized in Table 1.

Study 2—Shape Specification

The objective was to measure the extrafoveal similarity of a set of five shapes. We also wanted to study how other variables (size, con-

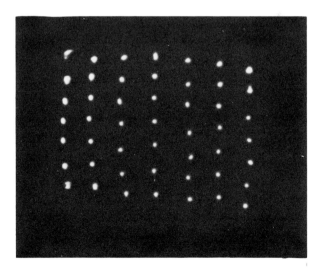

FIGURE 4   A calibration matrix—49 fixations.

TABLE 1 Proportion of Fixations on Objects Having the Specified Characteristics[a]

| Specified Characteristics | Correctly Fixated Characteristics | | | | | | | | | | | | | |
| | Color | | | | | Size (degrees of visual angle) | | | | Shape | | | | |
	Bl	Gr	Ye	Or	Pi	2.8	1.9	1.3	.8	Ci	Sc	Tr	Sq	Cr
Color	.61	.56	.59	.71	.60									
Size						.59	.29	.28	.35					
Shape										.26	.24	.24	.23	.29
Color + size	.59	.65	.67	.66	.59	.52	.30	.30	.30					
Color + shape	.64	.64	.66	.59	.59					.24	.26	.27	.24	.28
Size + shape						.57	.30	.29	.35	.27	.25	.26	.24	.30
Color + size + shape	.54	.55	.55	.62	.54	.49	.31	.29	.28	.26	.28	.25	.26	.26
Number only	.20	.20	.20	.18	.22	.25	.25	.26	.24	.20	.20	.20	.20	.20

[a]To illustrate, when color-plus-size was specified, then for yellow targets 67 percent of the fixations were on yellow objects. When color alone was specified, then for yellow targets 59 percent of the fixations were on yellow objects. The bottom row shows the proportion of fixations on objects of each characteristic indicated by the column label when only the two-digit number was specified.

trast, and object density) affected similarity. When all objects were the same size or contrast, we expected that the extrafoveal discriminability of their shape would be greater than it was when they varied in size or contrast.

The target was specified by its shape. Each object in the field other than the target contained a three-digit number. However, for the target, the middle digit was replaced by the letter T (for example, the target might contain the label 3T5). The fields differed in density of objects (either 40 or 100 objects were in the field) contrast of objects (all objects were high contrast, all low contrast, or a mixture of high and low), and size of objects (all objects were large, all small, or a mixture of large and small). Thus, there were 18 different types of fields. Figure 5 is one such field.

The overall similarities are shown in Table 2. If these results are compared with the data from the other studies, it will be seen that these values are higher, implying that it is harder to use shape information than size or color, for example.

Some symmetry is apparent. Thus, the similarity of one shape to a second was about the same as the similarity of the second shape to the first.

Similarity was completely unaffected by density. Homogeneity of size and contrast, however, increased discriminability somewhat (Table 3), since the average similarity of other objects to the target was reduced from .58 to .50 for homogeneous fields.

Study 3—Size Specification

The main objective was to measure similarity over a range of sizes. The main question is: How does the size difference between an object and the target affect their similarity? We also studied the effects of other variables relating to field composition, namely (a) the overall size range of the objects in the field, (b) the average size of the objects, (c) the magnitude of the increments in size of different objects (for example, in some fields the objects are relatively similar in size, as compared with other fields), and (d) contrast (fields contain either high contrast object, low contrast objects, or a mixture of high and low contrast objects).

Each field contained squares of either five or nine different sizes

FIGURE 5   A search field—shape study.

with increments in length of 22 percent for the small increment fields and increments of 50 percent for the large increment fields. The target was identifiable by a vertical patterning of dots, with all other objects having a horizontal pattern. The types of size compositions are shown in Figure 6.

Typical results are shown in Figure 7 for the WIDE-5 condition. Here a discrimination *gradient* can be seen. The greater the difference in size between an object and the target, the less likely will that object be fixated. This is true for all field types. Two more examples are shown in Figures 8 and 9. The slopes of the gradients were constant, with one exception. In other words, the similarity

TABLE 2   Similarities for Five Shapes

Specified Target Shape	Fixated Object				
	Circle	Semicircle	Triangle	Square	Rectangle
Circle	1.00	.54	.35	.41	.41
Semicircle	.66	1.00	.62	.59	.62
Triangle	.35	.50	1.00	.53	.56
Square	.50	.61	.64	1.00	.82
Rectangle	.39	.52	.58	.74	1.00

of a given size object to the target depended only on the ratio of the two sizes. It did *not* depend on the size of the target, on the range of sizes within a field, or the average size of objects within the field. In fact, similarity here was symmetrical, since the similarity of one size to a second was the same as the similarity of the second size to the first. Targets that were the largest objects in the field were an exception to this rule; however, the gradient between these targets and other objects in the field was considerably steeper than the other gradients, implying that they are more discriminable than other sizes of targets. The contrast composition within a field was found to have little effect on object similarity.

The overall conclusion from the study is that there is a discrimination gradient for size that is relatively unaffected by other measurable characteristics of the field. The mean gradients averaged over the three main size ranges are shown in Figure 10. Note that the gradients for the largest targets are *not* included in these averages.

Study 4—Color

The objective was to measure similarities for a set of colors in the Munsell color space. Each field contained 6 chips of each of 13 colors

TABLE 3   Mean Similarity of Other Shapes to Target for the Nine Field Types

Size of Objects in Field	Contrast of Objects in Field		
	All High	Mixed—High and Low	All Low
All large	.46	.56	.49
Mixed—large and small	.58	.58	.61
All small	.51	.58	.53

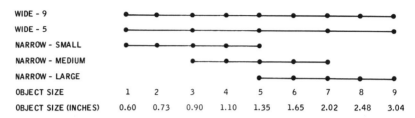

FIGURE 6   The five size ranges (solid circles on horizontal line indicate sizes of objects within each field).

on a neutral (value = 5.5) background. The target was identified by its trapezoidal shape, whereas the other 5 chips of target color and the 72 chips of other color were parallelograms. A Macbeth Skylight simulating north sky daylight at $6800°$ K provided the illumination. Two achromatic and 46 chromatic targets were used.

The results summarized in Figure 11 show the mean similarities of various neighboring colors to the target color averaged over all chromatic targets. A gradient for hue is apparent. Here a distance of five Munsell hue steps resulted in a similarity of less than .50, while 10

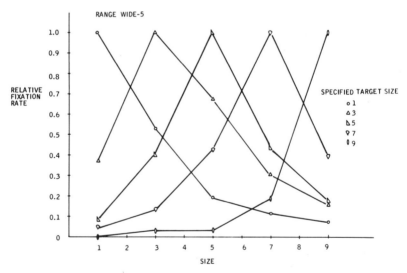

FIGURE 7   Discrimination gradients for WIDE-5 range.

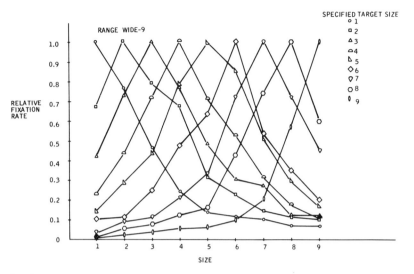

FIGURE 8   Discrimination gradients for WIDE-9 range.

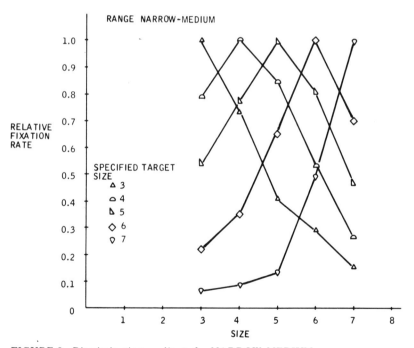

FIGURE 9   Discrimination gradients for NARROW–MEDIUM range.

Munsell steps reduces similarity to about .25. Twenty Munsell steps resulted in still lower similarity. The data in Figure 11 are a good representation of the entire space. The only qualification is that targets of higher Chroma had somewhat steeper gradients than those of lower Chroma.

Study 5–Lightness

The objective was to measure similarities over a set of neutral gray Munsell chips. Munsell value (i.e., lightness) was treated much the same as size in Study 3 in that we also studied the effects of the range of value within a field (chips varied in value from 1.5 to 9.5 in some fields and from 3.5 to 7.5 in others). Background lightness was also varied, and the Munsell values used were 1.5, 3.5, 5.5. 7.5, and 9.5.

Each field contained 10 chips of target value and 10 chips of each of 7 other values. As in the color study, the target was identified by its trapezoidal shape, the remaining chips being parallelograms. A pair of Macbeth Examolites were used for illumination.

The results were similar to those in the size study. For any target

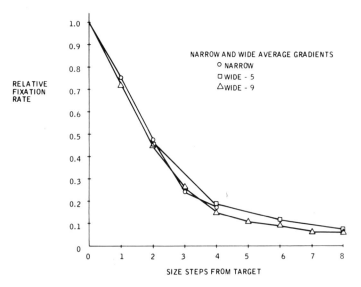

FIGURE 10   Average gradients for the three size ranges.

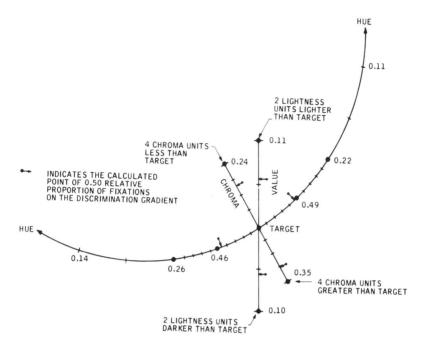

FIGURE 11   Average discrimination gradients for 46 chromatic targets.

value there was a clear discrimination gradient—the more different in value an object was from the target, the less often was it fixated. The gradient averaged over all targets is shown in Figure 12. The steepness of the gradient does not appear to depend on the value range, but there does seem to be a dependence on background value. Namely, when the target was most different from the background (i.e., when the target contrast was high) the gradient was steep. However, when the target was very similar to the background (i.e., its contrast was low) the gradient was also relatively steep. This latter result may appear surprising.

CONCLUSIONS

The basic result is that when searching for targets subjects tend to fixate objects having the target specifications. When a specified target characteristic is on a continuum (e.g., size or value), a gradient

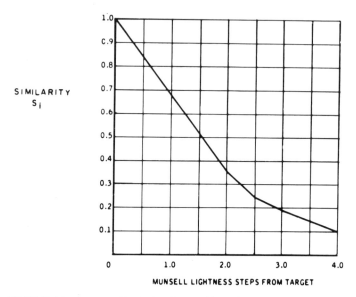

FIGURE 12   Average discrimination gradients for neutral gray
targets.

of discrimination is found. This gradient is, by and large, independent of field characteristics such as object density, differences between objects other than those directly relating to the target specification, and the range of variation along the relevant target dimension.
Targets at the high extreme of a continuum (e.g., largest or of greatest
contrast) are most discriminable from other objects.

REFERENCES

Williams, L. G., A study of visual search using eye movement recordings. Honeywell, Inc., Document 12009-IR 1, 1966.
Williams, L. G., A study of visual search using eye movement recordings. Honeywell, Inc., Document 12009-IR 2, 1967.

HARRY L. SNYDER*
THE BOEING COMPANY

Modulation Transfer Function Area as a Measure of Image Quality

In accordance with the principles of good systems engineering, the designer of any imaging or viewing system should bear in mind the needs and capabilities of the observer along with the tasks required of the observer, whether the system of interest is a simple optical aid, a combination of a camera, film, and projector, or an electronically complex low-light-level electrooptical device. Unfortunately, the past decade has seen the development of highly sophisticated photographic and electrooptical reconnaissance systems designed for a myriad of uses, only to find that the observer of the imagery produced is unable to obtain the proper information from the imagery within the alotted time.

Many of the problems in operational use of such systems have been attributed to the gross incompatibility between the quality (and often the quantity) of imagery produced and the capabilities and limitations of the observer. Several experiments have been conducted (e.g., Brainard *et al.*, 1966) in an effort to define parametric relationships between characteristics of the design of imaging systems and the viewer's performance in interpreting the image. In a review of over 300 related reports (Snyder, 1967), it was pointed out that numerous

*Present address: Department of Industrial Engineering and Operations Research, Virginia Polytechnic Institute and State University.

conflicts exist in experimental results and that the designer of electro-optical systems, for example, still has no coherent body of data that will specify how he can make his design compatible with the observer's visual capabilities. This problem still exists, although some progress has been made, as in Biberman *et al.* (1970).

In order to reduce the number of relationships between performance of the interpreter and measures of image quality, several studies have attempted to find a summary measure of image quality, one to which many design variables might be reduced. For example, Brainard *et al.* (1966) found a multiple correlation of 0.60 between several physical measures of quality of photographic images and performance in identifying targets. The physical measures included absolute acutance, absolute resolution, ground resolution, and scale. At the same time, Borough *et al.* (1967) were obtaining data on a summary measure of image quality, the modulation transfer function area (MTFA). In the Borough *et al.* study, judgments of image quality, based on a partial paired-comparison scaling technique, were correlated with MTFA values. They demonstrated a strong relationship, but no data on interpretation performance were obtained. The relationships arrived at by Brainard *et al.* and by Borough *et al.* are shown in Figure 1.

The strong promise of the MTFA measure, as demonstrated by Borough *et al.*, coupled with the applicability of MFTA to electronic and electrooptical imaging systems of a wide variety led Boeing to collect the information extraction performance data required to complete the bottom triangle of Figure 1. This paper, then, reports the recently completed results of that study, performed by Dr. C. L. Klingberg, Dr. C. L. Elworth, and Mr. C. R. Filleau.*

METHOD

Imagery Preparation

The imagery used in this experiment was the same as that of Borough *et al.* (1967) and will be described only briefly here. Nine reconnais-

*The research was sponsored by the Air Force Office of Scientific Research under Contract Number F 44620-69-C-0128.

sance photographs were selected for quality modification; the scenes contained such items as petroleum storage tanks, harbor facilities, industrial complexes, ships, dams, airfields, and drive-in theaters. All were vertical photos and ranged in displayed scale from 1:3750 to 1:240000.

Original negatives were used to produce 32 negative copies varying in contrast, granularity, and modulation transfer function, as shown in Figure 2. The three contrast levels were 41:1, 14:1, and 2.75:1. The three levels of grain noise were .022, .43, and .61 rms. The four MTF curves are illustrated in Figure 3.

The modulation transfer function (MTF) simply defines the percent original contrast that is transmitted by a system as a function of the spatial "closeness" of two elements in the original object plane. For a general discussion of the MTF concept, see Jensen (1968).

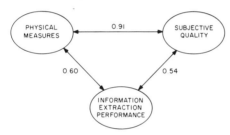

RESULTS FROM BRAINARD, ET AL. (1966)

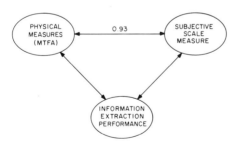

RESULTS FROM BOROUGH, ET AL. (1967)

FIGURE 1   Correlations between physical measures of image quality, subjective image quality, and information extraction performance.

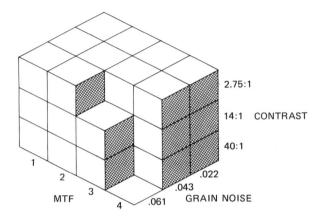

FIGURE 2   Thirty-two combinations of variables affect-
ing image quality.

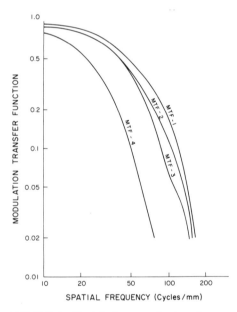

FIGURE 3   Modulation transfer functions as
measured by edge-response method.

From these combined values of granularity, contrast, and MTF, a total of 36 (3 × 3 × 4) MTFA values was calculated. Four MTFA values were eliminated from further use due to numerical duplication; hence, 32 cells remain in Figure 2.

The MTFA is simply the area bounded by the system MTF curve, some arbitrary low-frequency cutoff (if used), and the detection threhsold curve for the combination of the human observer and the and the imaging system (Figure 4). In the present experiment, the MTF curve is given by the experimental conditions as shown in Figures 2 and 3. The low-frequency cutoff was taken to be 10 lines per millimeter when the MTF was calculated from a log–log plot, and no cutoff was used when the MTF was plotted on linear axes. The use of a cutoff frequency on the log–log plot merely serves to de-emphasize the low frequencies, which otherwise heavily weighted in the MTFA integral on a log-log plot.

The detection-threshold curve is based on the contrast threshold curve of the observer and the grain noise of the film. Figure 5 illustrates the components of the detection-threshold curve. The flat portion at the lower spatial frequencies is merely the assumed contrast threshold of the eye (.04 at $\gamma = 1.0$). The system gamma, if greater than unity, enhances the modulation recorded on the film (or display) so that the minimum detectable image-modulation decreases by $.04/\gamma$. Following Scott (1963), the threshold de-

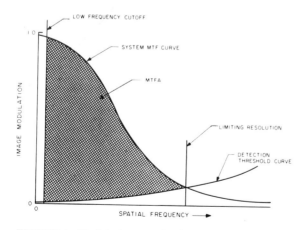

FIGURE 4   Modulation transfer function area (MTFA).

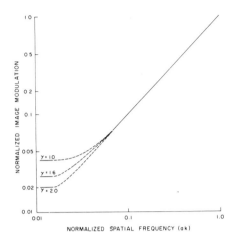

FIGURE 5   Generalized detection threshold curve.

tection curve is positioned vertically by increasing the ordinate by $M_t(ak)/M_o$, where $M_t(ak)$ is the generalized value as shown in Figure 5, and M_o is the object contrast-modulation. The curve is then positioned horizontally by multiplying the scale of the abscissa in Figure 5 by $\gamma/C\sigma(D)$, where γ is the gamma of the system, C is an empirically derived constant of .03 (for fine-grained films such as Type 4404) or .04 (for coarse-grained films, such as Plus-X or Tri-X), and $\sigma(D)$ is rms granularity.

Thus, the system MTF is rigorously defined in the absence of noise, whereas the detection-threshold curve includes all display, environment, and visual capability factors.

Subjective Image Quality

The aforementioned study by Borough *et al.* (1967) produced the calculated MTFA values for each of the 32 variants of the nine scenes, along with scaled subjective estimates of image quality. Figure 6 indicates the range of MTFA values for each of the nine scenes. Using a partial paired-comparison scaling technique (256 pairs per subject rather than 496 pairs and a total of 36 trained photointerpreters), scalar values were defined for each of the 288 (9 × 32) photographs.

Interpreter Performance

Elworth and Klingberg (1969) tested a total of 384 trained military photointerpreters for information extraction from the 288 photographs. Each subject was given one variant of each of the nine scenes and asked to (a) rank order the nine scenes for their relative potential for extracting intelligence data without regard to scale, subject matter, and content; (b) assign a position on a 9-point interpretability scale to each of the nine photos; and (c) answer eight multiple-choice questions regarding content, location, mensuration, and other important features of each photograph. Thus, each subject could make as many as 72 (9 × 8) errors on the interpretability portion of the test, while each of the 288 image variants was examined by 12 (384 × 9/288) Ss. Equivalently, a total of 96 (12 Ss, 8 questions) errors could be made on each of the 288 image variants. The sources of the subject population are analyzed in Table 1.

RESULTS

Interpreter Performance

Figure 7 indicates the distribution of errors for the 32 variants of each photograph. While some scenes and questions were clearly more difficult than others, there is no suggestion of severe attenuation or skewness to the error distributions for any of the scenes.

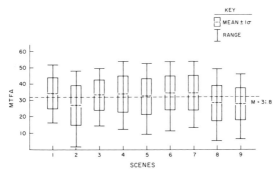

FIGURE 6 MTFA values for the nine scenes.

TABLE 1   Description of Subject Sample

Source	Air Force		Army		Navy		Marine		Total		
	C[a]	NC[b]	C	NC	C	NC	C	NC	C	NC	Σ
U.S. Army Intelligence School	–	–	30	61[c]	–	–	–	6	30	67	97
U.S.A.F. Intelligence School	117[d]	131	–	–	31	5	3	–	151	136	287
Totals	248		91		36		9		181	203	384

[a]Commissioned Officer.
[b]Noncommissioned Officer.
[c]Includes 1 female.
[d]Includes 12 females.

The error-distribution by subject-type is given in Table 2. No significant differences were found in comparisons of schools, services, or commissioned status.

Intercorrelations

Figure 8 shows a scatter plot of the MTFA for each of the 32 variants, summed across scenes, against information extraction performance. The product-moment correlation between MTFA and performance is −.93.

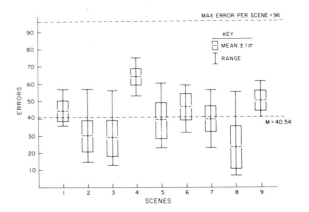

FIGURE 7   Interpretation error distributions for the nine scenes.

TABLE 2 Mean Errors per Subject

Source	Air Force		Army		Navy		Marine		Total		M̄
	C	NC	C	NC	C	NC	C	NC	C	NC	
U.S. Army Intelligence School	–	–	31.2	30.2	–	–	–	31.2	31.2	30.3	30.6
U.S.A.F. Intelligence School	30.1	30.9	–	–	28.7	28.0	28.0	–	29.8	30.8	30.3
Totals	30.5		30.6		28.6		30.5		30.1	30.6	30.4

Figure 9 illustrates the relationship ($r = -.96$) between the image quality scaled-value obtained by Klingberg *et al.* (1970) and the MTFA values measured by Borough *et al.* (1967). It should be noted that this correlation of –.96 is equivalent to the correlation obtained by Borough *et al.* (.93). The sign of the correlation is, of course, irrelevant and varies only because of assignment of high or low scale numbers to "good" photographs.

On a scene-by-scene basis, these correlations are given in Table 3, which also indicates that the product-moment correlation between information extraction performance and subjective scaling by the

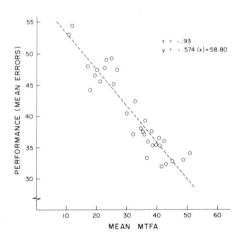

FIGURE 8 Correlation between MTFA and information extraction performance.

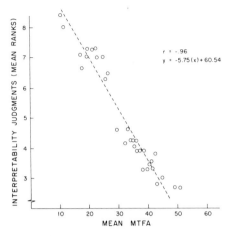

FIGURE 9   Correlation between MTFA and subjective image quality as determined by ranking method.

ranking method is .97. As a further check on agreement between the partial paired-comparison technique of Borough *et al.* and the ranking/absolute judgment method of Klingberg *et al.*, a correlation of .97 was obtained between the two sets of subjective scalar values. Intercorrelations of this type, on a scene-by-scene basis, are shown in Table 4.

DISCUSSION

The data from these studies point out the highly promising nature of MTFA as a useful summary measure of image quality. Whether MTFA, MTF, $(MTF)^2$, Schade's N_e (Schade, 1953), or some other similar

TABLE 3   Correlations (Pearson r's) between Image Quality, Interpreter Performance, and Subjective Judgments

	Scene									$\bar{r}$ [a]	r_m [b]
	1	2	3	4	5	6	7	8	9		
$r$perf./MTFA	.69	.66	.80	.65	.78	.55	.84	.86	.46	.72	.93
$r$perf./rank	.71	.67	.89	.60	.80	.42	.78	.76	.42	.70	.97
rMTFA/rank	.90	.87	.90	.93	.94	.87	.92	.86	.83	.90	.96

N = 32 image quality levels (MTFA).
[a] $\bar{r}$ = Average of r's using Z scores.
[b] r_m = Values averaged across scenes before computing correlation.

TABLE 4   Scene-by-Scene Intercorrelations

	R	M	V	R	M	V	R	M	V
	Scene 1			Scene 2			Scene 3		
Perf (P)	.71	.69	.68	.67	.66	.67	.89	.80	.83
Ranks (R)		.90	.92		.87	.87		.90	.91
MTFA (M)			.92			.93			.88
P-C values (V)			–			–			–
	Scene 4			Scene 5			Scene 6		
Perf (P)	.60	.65	.64	.80	.78	.76	.42	.55	.70
Ranks (R)		.93	.92		.94	.92		.87	.83
MTFA (M)			.92			.93			.92
P-C values (V)			–			–			–
	Scene 7			Scene 8			Scene 9		
Perf (P)	.78	.84	.82	.76	.86	.82	.42	.46	.43
Ranks (R)		.92	.90		.86	.87		.83	.77
MTFA (M)			.92			.92			.91
P-C values (V)			–			–			–
All Scenes Combined									
Perf (P)	.97	.93	.93						
Ranks (R)		.96	.97						
MTFA			.97						
P-C values			–						

metric is the best single predictor for *all* imaging systems is certainly unsettled at this time. However, these results indicate that for typical photographic image quality and for a non-time-limited observer, the MTFA measures becomes an extremely valid predictor of relative information extraction performance.

One of the advantages of the MTFA is that it lends itself to analytical prediction at an early stage in the design of any imaging system. Further, it is easily verified in the laboratory when the detection-threshold curve is known. Specification of the detection-threshold curve for *representative viewing conditions* is, however, not totally straightforward. The eye's contrast threshold varies not only with spatial frequency but also with image signal-to-noise level and with such environmental variables as glare, vibration, and adaptation-level.

An MTFA analysis can also be applied to nonphotographic imaging systems, such as radar, infrared, and television. Although such systems rarely produce the same order of resolution as photographic systems in lines per millimeter on the display, interesting results are obtained when such systems are equated for display scale. For example, the MTF plots used in the imagery of this study fall exactly in the middle of typical MTF plots of current low-light-level television systems if the abscissa is modified to become cycles per ground unit rather than cycles per display unit. Whether the MTFA measures will yield as high a performance prediction for such electrooptical systems as it has for photographic systems remains an empirical question.

A further note with regard to electrooptical systems is that the MTF is defined specifically in the absence of noise, so that at low sensor irradiance (and hence low S/N levels), a display may have considerable "snow" and thereby produce poor information-extraction performance even though the system MTF remains unchanged. For this reason, it is most important that the display S/N level be included as a determinant of the threshold-detection curve used in the MTFA calculations and that other conditions under which the MTFA is defined (e.g., display luminance and operating environment) also be specified to avoid ambiguity. Clearly, much research is needed before the MTFA can be used universally for all imaging-system specifications.

REFERENCES

Biberman, L. M., A. D. Schnitzler, F. A. Rosell, and H. L. Snyder. Low Light Level Devices: A Manual for Systems Designers Who Care. Report R-169, Institute for Defense Analyses, July 1970.

Borough, H. C., R. F. Fallis, T. H. Warnock, and J. H. Britt. Quantitative Determination of Image Quality. The Boeing Company Report D2-114058-1, May 1967.

Brainard, R. W., R. Sadacca, L. J. Lopez, and G. N. Ornstein. Development and Evaluation of a Catalog Technique for Measuring Image Quality. U.S. Army Personnel Office Report 1150, August 1966.

Elworth, C. L., and C. L. Klingberg. Image Quality and Detection Performance of Military Interpreters. The Boeing Company Document D162-10323-1, 1969.

Jensen, N. Optical and Photographic Reconnaissance Systems. Wiley, New York, 1968.

Schade, O. H. Image gradation, graininess, and sharpness in television and motion-picture systems. Part III: The grain structure of television images. J. Soc. Motion Pict. Telev. Eng., 61, 97–163, 1953.

Scott, F. Image Evaluation for Reconnaissance, Proceedings of a Symposium. Itek Co. Report 9048-6, April 1963.

Snyder, H. L. Low Light Level TV Viewfinder Simulation Program. Phase A: State-of-the-Art Review. (SECRET). USAF Report AFAL-TR-67-293, November 1967.

JOHN W. SENDERS
BRANDEIS UNIVERSITY

Visual Scanning Behavior

A DISCUSSION OF ATTENTION

One man understands what another means when he says either that he gave his attention to something or that something caught his attention. If something *catches* your attention, you attend to it, that is, focus on it and examine it. Perhaps the *giving* of attention prior to its being caught is a different phenomenon, one in which the incentive comes from within rather than from without. In either event, the process ends with an examination of the thing attended to. During the process of examination, one assumes that attention is being "given" to the object; in a sense, though, it is the transition from switching of attention from one object to another that is the most manifest characteristic of attention.

For certain classes of sequences of events that demand attention from the observer, the frequency of this demand can be estimated. The magnitude of the demand can be estimated both on the basis of objective physical characteristics of the time series of events and of subjective states and characteristics of the observer. The product of the frequency and magnitude of the demand will be a measure of the "attentional demand" made by that information source, or signal, on the observer.

In this paper, attention will be considered to be unitary and capa-

106

ble of dealing with only one demand at a time. The frequency with which it can alternate between various time series of events may be sufficiently high that apparent simultaneity of processing will be observed. Whether apparent simultaneity will be observed is calculable on the basis of the physical characteristics of the time series involved. Looked at in this light, the attention of an observer may be considered to be a channel processing in sequence, never simultaneously, information arriving from many outside sources.

What might be the basis on which an information source demands attention from an observer or, alternatively, the basis on which an observer decides to direct his attention to an information source? It is reasonable to treat these as examples of the same general process; this process is reduction of uncertainty. In other words, the observer who voluntarily directs his attention to some information source does so in order to reduce his uncertainty about the nature of the information presented. This uncertainty could arise in one of two ways. First, if the information source (a place in the visual field) is dynamic and time-varying, uncertainty as to the value of the variable presented must have accumulated since the last observation of that source; and, second, even if the process is static and unchanging in time, there is an internal time-based change in the observer, i.e., forgetting, which results in an increase in uncertainty about the nature of the information displayed. As the observer forgets, he does not instantaneously become totally uncertain about the nature of the thing he has seen. Instead, there appears in the observer merely an increase in the range of values that might be identified as the one previously seen. Such an increase in the range of possible values could be computed as an increase in entropy or uncertainty. There is no reason for treating this internal growth in entropy as different from the entropy of an external source of information. Thus, the observer attends to the information source whenever the uncertainty as to the value presented exceeds some critical level. From his point of view, the meaning of increasing uncertainty, whether internally or externally generated, depends entirely on what the observer is trying to do. If the observer is continually interested in the magnitude of a time-varying process, then his behavior will be quite different from that which will be exhibited by someone engaged in "check-reading." The former person is doing a quantitative read-out of the magnitude of the process at every moment in time. The latter person is engaged in making a three-part decision about the values, i.e., it is above acceptable limits, it is below acceptable limits, or it is within acceptable limits; and the numerical value of the item presented is not important. Furthermore, this latter observer will have some cost associated with the act of observing and will have some cost associated with a value outside acceptable limits. These give rise to a calculable threshold probability for the observer. Then he will observe when the probability of going outside of acceptable limits has exceeded that threshold value.

Further complications may exist if there is some probability distribution of acceptable limits instead of sharp, well-defined upper and lower limits, and if, instead of some arbitrary probability of exceeding acceptable limits, there is some variable probability. However, for the most part these complications give rise merely to increases in the complexity of the calculation rather than to changes in the forms of the equations.

If an observer had only one information source to tend to and if literally no distracting or attention-demanding internal events occurred, then the probability of his detecting events of interest at that source would approach unity. That is to say, whenever that source required attention, it could be attended to without delay. On the other hand, if there exist two or more information sources, each demanding attention and uncorrelated with one another, then there exists a probability that simultaneous demand will occur. That is, the observer will be attending to one source and satisfying a requirement for uncertainty reduction when the other source demands attention. Under these conditions the second source must wait. If it must wait and if, as defined earlier, the probability of an event of importance has risen above some arbitrary value, then there is a finite probability that the event of interest will occur and will be missed. Thus, if there were N information sources, we could compute the probability of simultaneous demand upon the observer and, therefore, an overall probability that signals will be missed.

These notions of attentional demand are quite relevant to the behavior involved in piloting aircraft. Aircraft instruments are designed to provide pilots with information needed to control aircraft in flight, information such as the attitude of an aircraft, its location in three-dimensional space, and the rate of change of its attitude and location vectors. Knowledge of how pilots use their eyes when they are flying on instruments, i.e., how they obtain data from separate instruments in order to combine bits of discrete information into a total picture of "what the aircraft is doing," is fundamental to a basic understanding of the function served by aircraft instruments. Such knowledge should guide the engineer to design useful instruments. It can form a scientific basis for improving the design of aircraft instruments, increasing the efficiency of pilots, and simplifying the task of instrument flying (Jones *et al.*, 1946). These authors felt that frequency of eye fixations on any given instrument is an indication of the relative importance of that instrument. The length of fixations, on the contrary, may more properly be considered as an indication of the relative difficulty of checking and interpreting particular instruments. The pattern of eye movements, i.e., the link values between instruments, is a direct indication of how well the panel is arranged.

APPROACHES TO VISUAL SAMPLING

A brief discussion of various approaches to modeling human visual sampling behavior follows. Details of these models may be found in other sources (Carbonell, 1966; Senders *et al.*, 1965; Smallwood, 1966).

Periodic Sampling

In previous reports (Senders, 1955, 1958), I have considered a human monitor of some large number of informational displays. A theoretical model was suggested based on the assumption that the task of the monitor was to reconstruct the time functions (i.e., the instrument reading) presented on each of the displays. As a result, it was possible to present equations based on the assumption of periodic sampling, which predicted quite well the mean behavior of experimental subjects in a highly constrained laboratory situation (Senders, 1964).

I (Senders, 1955, 1958, 1964) attempted to apply a very much simplified sampling theory to human scanning behavior. A great many assumptions were made in arriving at the simple solutions, and these would not be justified in many real situations. The ideal observer was assumed to be interested in reading out, or reconstructing, the signal on the basis of the samples that he had taken. If this assumption holds, the calculations based on it will be valid. However, most real observers engaged in real tasks are not concerned with signal reconstruction. Instead the observer attempts only to be aware of a departure of the signal from some arbitrarily chosen amount. That is to say, as mentioned briefly earlier, most real observers are engaged in "check-reading." The data presented in Senders (1964) show remarkably good approximation to the theoretical values. This was particularly so for the transition probabilities and was sufficiently close for the sampling frequencies themselves to permit useful estimation of the "attentional demand" imposed by each of the four independent signals used in the experiment. The observer's task, however, was not in fact the task of signal reconstruction. Instead it was a check-reading task. The data conform because the powers of the signals and the magnitudes of the significant deviations were the same for all signals. There was a logical necessity, therefore, for the sampling frequencies to be proportional to the bandwidths, and in fact the data were in accord with this prediction. It was not pointed out in that earlier paper (Senders, 1964) that if the powers had not been equal or, given that the powers were equal, if the magnitudes of the significant deviations were not equal, then the sampling frequencies would not have been proportional to the bandwidths. It is, however, constructive to follow the original reasoning because the operators are in fact engaged in the reading of signals under certain operational conditions. The theory holds quite well for these conditions, and, in a sense, the behavior of the subjects is forced. [Detailed mathematical analyses can be found in Senders (1966).]

Transitional Probabilities (Link Values)

As a consequence of the sampling performed by the observer on the various instruments of a set, transitions will be made from one instrument to another and frequency distributions of such transitions will be generated. We can examine the consequences of the assumption that the sequence of transitions is a random series constrained only by the relative frequencies of fixation of the instruments involved in any transition. We assume that a transition starting from instrument *i* may end on any instrument, including instrument *i*, in accord with the probabilities of fixation on each instrument. Over a sufficiently long time-interval, the relative number of fixations on each instrument will be an estimate of the probability of fixation on that instrument, and this, in turn, reduces to the equating of the relative frequency of fixation to the probability of fixation.

It is clear that if the probabilities of a fixation on two signals are large, many transitions will perforce be made between them. However, it is also obvious that, as the probabilities of the various instruments approach equality, the freedom of path through the set of instruments increases and is greatest when all are equal. Thus, as the restraints of relative frequency diminish, there is greater opportunity for logical patterns of scanning. Either by applying the models for sampling strategies to hypothetical or known signals or by direct measurement of the relative times spent observing the various display devices in a man–machine system, we can arrive at useful estimates of the probability of fixation of each of the signal sources or instruments. The original series of pilot eye-movement studies in 1953 and 1954 was aimed at determining by direct measurements the various fixation probabilities and using them to determine the locations of the instruments then commonly used.

In addition to measuring fixation probabilities, these studies also determined the successive pairs of instruments fixated. The goal was to establish "links" between instruments that could act as a basis for arranging instruments. Here again the utility of the estimated transition probabilities is apparent: The greater the probability of transition between two signals, the closer together they should be.

My model for the transition process treats the observer as if he drew at random from the set of displayed signals with probabilities equal to the fixation probabilities each time a transition is made. Such an observer would make transitions between instruments without regard for any real or imagined relation between signals displayed. Although I do not contend that pilots in fact behave this way in aircraft, it is nonetheless true that the predictions of the model are in close enough accord with the actual link vaues measured in flight to have served as a basis for decisions on the layout of instrument panels.

The predictions of the model and the results of laboratory studies (Lindquist and Gross, 1958; Senders, 1964) agree even more closely, and the agreement is close enough that the model can account for nearly all of the behavior observed in the laboratory.

The laboratory data were gathered on a set of random, unrelated signals. Thus there would be no basis for selection other than the probability of fixation itself. A deviation on one instrument was not indicative of the signal that might be observed on any other. In an aircraft, on the other hand, there would be two processes that would determine the next item to be selected by the observer. If the prior observation found the signal inside the acceptable region, then the selection of a signal for the succeeding observation could be made on a properly weighted random basis. If the prior observation were of a significant deviation, then the coupling that existed between the displayed signals would lead to a rational selection of an instrument that might be presumed to be related to the observed deviation, e.g., if altitude were "off," then rate of descent would be a reasonable thing to look at. Our expectation, therefore, should be that the demands estimated by the simple model will only partially describe the sampling behavior of the pilot and that this description will be of those signals that have the highest probabilities of fixation.[*]

For the situation with equal signal powers and equal significant deviations, the foregoing is an adequate description and can be used (although with caution) in the analysis of real systems. However, the estimates that can be made are only estimates of the means of distribution of intervals between observations. There is nothing that permits an estimate of the variability of these distributions.

That there are distributions is apparent both from the data and from purely logical considerations. Aperiodicity in the sampling of any one instrument would result from almost any configuration of instruments and bandwidths except for rare cases in which

---

*Since an instrument can be fixated and then refixated without an intervening eye movement, the measurable frequencies and durations of observation will not be those that would have been calculated on the basis of signal bandwidths and accuracy requirements, but the distributions will be modified as a result of the possibility of these successive fixations. [See Senders (1964) for detailed discussion.]

all the signals had identical bandwidths and identical significant deviations.

Faced with the observed data about the distributions of durations both of observations and of interobservation intervals, one is led to attempt to account for these distributions in a rational rather than in a descriptive way. The basis of this approach is that the interval between observations is a function of the value previously read, and the duration of an observation is a function of the value then being read by the observer. A discussion of this model follows.

Conditional Aperiodic Sampling

Let us consider the problem faced by a monitor of limited channel capacity confronted with many more than two signals to attend to but concerned with detection of extreme readings rather than with reconstruction of the signal. Such a monitor may serve not as a channel for the transmission of a complete time function but rather as a channel for the transmission of discrete pulses in time, i.e., as a channel for the transmission of a dichotomized (or polychotomized) time function or signal. For any function, one might assume that there is a limit-value that calls for the transmission of a message and that all values of the function below this limit call for no transmission of the message. This is analogous to stating that the monitor observes the time functions and does nothing so long as they remain within a "safe" interval. When a function exceeds the limits of safe operation, the monitor emits a signal that may be the present value of the function. We may now ask what the appropriate sampling strategy will be for the monitor. How accurately must the function be read if signals are to be sent properly? It is easy to see that if the permissible error, between the function as presented and the function as read, is equal to the amplitude of the function, no observation is needed. Similarly, if the permissible error approaches zero, then the information to be absorbed per sample increases and a longer time will be required for the monitor to accept and transmit the information. What is the proper strategy for selection of an interval between observations? If the function at the moment of observation has a value zero (i.e., its mean), then the next sample may be deferred until such time τ as the probability of the function's exceeding the limits of safe operation exceeds some arbitrarily set probability. In particular, if the limit of safe operation is some N standard deviations, then, as τ increases, the correlation decreases, the variance increases, and there will come a point where the probability of the function's exceeding the limit is equal to or greater than the arbitrarily set probability. At that point a sample would be taken. If the function, at the time of original observation, is greater than zero, i.e., is some fraction of the way toward the permissible N standard deviation, then the point at which the probability reaches or exceeds the arbitrarily chosen probability will in general come sooner, and the sample must be taken after a shorter interval. In the limit, as the observed value of the function approaches the N standard deviation, the acceptable sampling interval approaches zero.

The preceding description is reasonable for a monitoring (i.e., open-loop) task. Serious complications might arise when the observer is engaged in a control (i.e., closed-loop) task, in which the closer he controls, the smaller are the observed deviations but the more often he may have to look at the instrument. Also, this description assumes one possible strategy: the probability threshold criterion (Senders *et al.,* 1965). Other sampling strategies might involve the sampling of the function at the moment when the probability of exceeding the permissible limit is a maximum, or sampling when that probability exceeds a certain threshold, or sampling according to a "variable signal bandwidth" rule [see Senders *et al.* (1965) for details]. The various strategies are not necessarily mutually exclusive. The actual process of "conditional sampling" is probably a combination of two or more strategies. Which mathematical model is best depends on the momentary goal of the observer.

Whatever model or set of models is chosen for the monitor, the deduced distributions can be inserted into a queueing model in which signals line up to await their turn for the attention of the observer. Using this notion as a beginning, queue statistics can be calculated and a more complete picture of the hypothetical behavior generated.

Queueing: A Model of Attention

I have suggested that an information source will, from time to time, demand attention from the observer and that the observer will "pay attention" to that information source if he can. Either on the basis of purely theoretical considerations or on the basis of actual observations of monitoring behavior, we could construct a probability distribution of attentional demands made by an information source. If it is assumed that demands are always separated by periods of attention, then the probability function has the value of zero at $\tau = 0$. In general, as τ increases (where it is time since last observation), the probability of a new demand increases to a maximum and then diminishes monotonically to zero. If it is conceivable that an information source would demand attention on a completely periodic basis, the distribution for that source would merely be an impulse, $p = 1$, at some interval τ. In general, however, information sources will demand attention at intervals that depend on characteristics of the sources and of the observer's task in using that source.

We can similarly calculate or measure the distribution of durations of attentive acts, or observations, of the various information sources. Observation takes time, so the probability of an observation of zero duration is zero. In general, the probability of any duration will increase with increasing duration to a maximum and then decline monotonically to zero at some duration. Again, if an information source were so constructed as to require a constant observation time, then the distribution would shrink to an impulse, $p = 1$, at that duration. For most information sources, there will be a distribution of durations of observations that will depend on the characteristics of the information source and the observer's task in using that source.

Since, in general, the intervals of demand will overlap the intervals of observation, one can compute the probability that there will be interference, i.e., the human observer will be busy observing one source when another source demands attention. As either of two events occur—an increase in the frequency with which demands are made by one or more sources or an increase in the duration of observation times, resulting perhaps from an increase in complexity of signal to be observed—the amount of interference will increase.

The value of the probability distribution and the observing distribution would, of course, be the same. The statement of the observing distribution is that we can see at this point a possibility of computing, on the basis of known characteristics of the information source, the distributions for each information source, as well as the probabilities that each of the information sources will be observed at all. Therefore, we can see an analytical solution to the calculation of the probability of simultaneous demand for certain classes of information sources. (The results of previous investigations on simultaneous listening, or simultaneous listening and looking, which suggest a "competition between sources as a function of the redundancy of predictability of the sources," agree fairly well with the results of this simple analysis.) See Senders *et al.* (1965) for a more rigorous calculation of the relationship between the information flow rate from each of the sources and the distributions of intervals of attentional demand and of durations of attending.

To recapitulate briefly, I assume that the operator or observer is a simple channel device and that demands are made on this device by sources of information in the environment; that the sources, in a sense, arrive at the single channel device and form a queue; and the length of the queue formed by the information sources at any time is a direct measure of the degree of interference that will exist in any experiment involving "simultaneous attending to two or more sources of information." The length of the queue is a distribution function. It can be calculated on the basis of the probability of simultaneous demand. The notion of the probability of simultaneous demand serves as the basis for a rational attack on questions of perceptual overload and of workload calculations. The various components of the theory advanced in Senders *et al.* (1965) were intended to apply to behavior in the limiting case where the operator is at peak loading and subject to potential overload. The questions raised by the underloaded case are more difficult to analyze and, for many practical applications, less important.

EXPERIMENTAL EVIDENCE

Early Queueing Model

Three experiments were designed to confirm earlier work (see Table 1 and Figure 1) by exploring the relationships between (a) signal bandwidth and frequency of duration, (b) required accuracy of reading and duration of observation, and (c) simultaneous variation of bandwidth and required accuracy of reading, on the one hand, and fre-

TABLE 1   Frequency of Fixation

	Signal Bandwidth					
	.64	.32	.16	.08	.04	.02
Subject 1	.504	.502	.265	.303	.215	.233
Corrected	1.024	.673	.297	.323	.222	.237
Subject 2	.639	.445	.423	.253	.263	.127
Corrected	1.298	.597	.485	.270	.272	.129
Mean	.572	.478	.344	.278	.239	.180
Corrected Mean	1.161	.635	.391	.297	.247	.183

quency and duration of observation, on the other—explored as concomitant rather than separated variables.

These experiments were specifically designed to

1. Measure the relationship between observation time and required accuracy of reading and compare these results with theortical predictions;

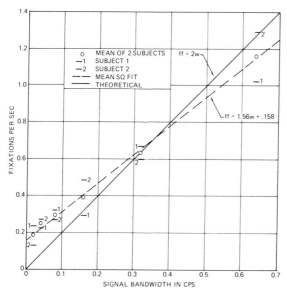

FIGURE 1   Experiment VI: Corrected frequency of fixation as a function of bandwidth in cps.

2. Measure the relationship between signal bandwidth and frequency of observation and compare these results with theoretical predictions;

3. Measure the effect of combined variations of bandwidth and required accuracy on frequency and duration of fixation and compare these results with the theoretical relationship obtained from the model equations;

4. Explore the relationship between the signal bandwidth and attention when the signal is quantized and displayed as a set of binary variables and fit these data to the theoretical model;

5. Explore the effects of signal dependency through correlation of signals and systems coupling.

Six signals, rather than the set of four instruments used in the 1953 and 1954 studies, were used in the monitoring tasks. Table 2 and Figure 1 present some of the general results, and more specific data relating to the five different experiments in this study can be found in Senders *et al.* (1965).

The general conclusion of this study, taken as a whole, is that the bandwidth of the monitored signal is the single most important factor influencing the frequency of fixation on that signal, granting that the power of the signal is set at some fixed level. The interaction between frequency of fixation and duration of fixation suggested by the simple Markov model was also strongly supported by the data taken as a whole as well as by the results of the individual experi-

TABLE 2 Observed and Simulated Eye Fixations in Percent for Three Pilots during Phase II of Flight (Turn)

		Pilot					
Instrument		P.M.		J.F.		D.M.	
No.	Name	Data	Model	Data	Model	Data	Model
1	Heading	19.6	15.4	22.7	21.7	25.0	27.9
3	Air speed	8.5	10.4	12.1	8.0	7.0	7.9
4	Altimeter	15.9	13.7	14.4	15.8	25.4	20.4
5 and 6	Pitch and roll	46.0	45.9	36.4	39.1	41.9	43.8
13	Rate of climb	10.0	14.6	14.4	15.4	.7	0
	Total	100.0	100.0	100.0	100.0	100.0	100.0

ments. The influence of reading accuracy on duration of fixation was still moot and remained for some future test. The simple Markov model also closely fits the data on observable frequency of fixation. However, this finding must be interpreted with caution. The data obtained in all these studies were relevant to a situation in which a number of indicators show signals that have nearly equal power, nearly identical "limits," no correlation (except for one instance), and no logical relationship between the readings on one indicator and the readings on another. In an operational space vehicle or aircraft, all of these conditions would be different for the various indicators. As a result, the more sophisticated notions of Senders *et al.* (1965) might be expected to afford better predictions of what the pilot will do in a monitoring task.

In general, the results of this study supported and reconfirmed the earlier four-instrument work. The difference between the earlier and later results, although suggesting that more sophisticated theory and experimentation were required, was not great enough to vitiate the applicability of the simple model. Later work done with a Link simulator gave us the opportunity to further extend our findings using a modified model.

Later Substantiation of New Queueing Model

The results of the previously mentioned series of experiments provided strong support for the hypothesis that observers are influenced by the bandwidths and accuracy requirements of the signals that they are to monitor. However, there were indeed failures of agreement between the models and the data, and these in turn led us to more sophisticated analyses of the determiners of the distribution of visual attention. Among these are the direct perception of visual rate, the assignment of differential costs to extreme deviations of different signals (Carbonell, 1966), the effect of nonveridical perception of the signal characteristics by the observer (Smallwood, 1966), and the effects of coupling and correlation between the various displayed signals (Senders *et al.*, 1968). The models of Carbonell (1966) and Smallwood (1966) have been tested by computer simulation against the earlier data obtained in 1954 and 1955 and reported in 1968 (Senders, 1968). Here it is possible to choose parameters such that

the behaviors exhibited by the models are well within the range of
those behaviors exhibited by human subjects. Thus, the first model
of 1955 appears to describe quite well the kinds of behavior that result when observers are required to monitor some relatively small
number of completely uncorrelated, bandlimited, normally distributed time functions and to report whenever any of these time
functions exceeds some symmetrically disposed, arbitrarily selected
limiting value (see Figure 1); Smallwood's model (the subjective one
of Smallwood, 1966) has resulted in a close approximation to the
actual behavior displayed by these subjects in the monitoring laboratory situation. Carbonell's model [the queueing model, Carbonell
(1966)] has given excellent approximation to visual sampling behavior in actual flight simulations. The ultimate utility of such models,
of course, may be twofold. On the other hand, they provide a basis for
examination of attentional mechanisms and for identifying the characteristics of the world of stimuli that actually serve to elicit observing responses on the part of observers, and, on the other hand, they
provide a potential means of estimating a number of paramaters relating to the way in which people will behave when confronted with
real tasks in real systems. For the moment it is this latter application
of the theory that concerns us. If these models (or any one of them)
hold true for controllers and monitors of real systems, then we can
calculate a number of things about such systems. Among these calculations would be the frequency with which the signal would be observed. This, of course, means that we can estimate in a statistical
way the interval between observations, their duration, and the sequences in which they would be made. We could, for example, calculate the probability that the monitor would in fact observe a transient
signal of any duration. Thus, some index of the "reliability" of the
human monitor in detecting signals could be obtained. In order to
accomplish all or even part of these ambitious goals we must show
that the behavior of human beings in real systems does in fact follow
the rules laid down by the models. Of course, most real systems are
markedly different from the systems that have ordinarily been used
in the laboratory. The differences are of the following kinds:

1. The signals presented on one instrument are very much related
to the signals presented on the other instruments, whereas in the
usual laboratory situation the signals were reported as unrelated;

2. The control process used by the system-controller modifies the short-term statistical characteristics of the signals, whereas in the monitoring laboratory situation the response activity of the monitor had no effect on the signal;

3. The distribution of signal values is non-Gaussian, whereas in the laboratory the signal is commonly constructed to be Gaussian;

4. The signal does not show a consistent tendency to regress to the mean, whereas in the laboratory the signal is usually assumed to have a mean value of zero;

5. There are no fixed arbitrary limits on each instrument, rather, these limits vary as a function of time depending on the immediate requirements of the machine and pilot and on the mission to which the combination is dedicated; on the other hand, in the laboratory the limits have usually been fixed and equal for all instruments.

For these reasons, it was felt necessary to perform more realistic experiments to avoid the oversimplifications of typical laboratory monitoring experiments. These experiments consisted in simultaneously recording both eye movements and panel instrument signals when experienced pilots were flying an instrumented landing approach flight in a Link simulator. An economic queueing model was designed to apply to the actual flight situation rather than the typical monitoring experiment.

An Economic Queueing Model of Visual Sampling

The main assumptions of this model are

1. The instruments compete for the pilot's attention; each time he looks at one instrument he is postponing the observation of others, which form a queue;

2. The queue discipline stems from an intelligent decision made by the pilot at each time; I assume that he tries to minimize the total risk involved in not observing the other instruments;

3. This risk is defined, for each instrument, as a unit cost times the probability that the displayed value may, while not being observed, exceed a certain threshold that could lead to some catastrophic result;

4. The pilot's task in visually sampling his instruments is part of a feedback loop closed through his control actions;

5. If the pilot does not exert control, displayed values are not zero-mean Gaussian signals, the mean will be given by the last reading of the instrument, and the variance will monotonically increase with time;

6. If the pilot exerts control, he will be concerned not with the absolute reading of each instrument but rather with variations from expected values.

In any actual implementation of the model, we are forced to make (by necessity) some further assumptions that are not, however, an intrinsic part of the model. Some of these are

7. The pilot looks at each instrument for a fixed length of time, namely .4 sec; longer looks are accounted for as consecutive selections of the same instruments in .4 sec units;

8. Control actions and autocorrelation functions of the signal are of the form exp $(-kt)$;

9. The divergence is accounted for by a linear term in τ subtracted from the square of the autocorrelation.

Results of Link Simulator Study

Senders *et al.* (1968) gives a complete analysis of the experimental conditions and the data. The general results of the simulation tests are presented here in Tables 3, 4, and 5, where both data and model results are normalized in percentages. Though pitch and roll are separate instruments in the model, they have been lumped together since they appear together on eye-movement data. The same is true for localizer and glidepath indicator.

The general agreement between pairs of data and model columns in Tables 3, 4, and 5 is surprisingly good. Table 3 refers to Phase II (turn) of the flight analyzed by the model, by pilot P. M. Table 4 presents results for the three pilots in Phase II; obviously Phase II by P. M. appears duplicated in Tables 3 and 4. Finally, Table 5 presents the results of the two simulation tests not covered in Tables 3 and 4.

TABLE 3   Observed and Simulated Eye Fixation in Percentages for a Given
Pilot (P. M.) during Three Different Phases of the Flight

Instrument		Phase I Beginning of Descent		Phase II Turn		Phase III Landing Approach	
No.	Name	Data	Model	Data	Model	Data	Model
1	Heading	18.2	16.3	19.6	15.4	22.4	14.6
3	Air speed	13.6	13.3	8.5	10.4	4.3	6.3
4	Altimeter	11.4	13.3	15.9	13.7	7.6	5.4
5 and 6	Pitch and roll	41.5	41.3	46.0	45.9	31.9	32.9
13	Rate of climb	15.3	15.8	10.0	14.6	8.6	14.2
14 and 15	Localizer and glide path	–	–	–	–	25.2	26.6
	Total	100.0	100.0	100.0	100.0	100.0	100.0

Next, Tables 6 to 8 present statistical analyses of the results already
presented in Tables 3, 4, and 5. Two types of statistical evaluation
have been applied. The first is simply the average of the absolute differences between predictions of the model and data expressed in percentages. The second is the ratio of the sum of the squares of the
differences between data and model (both in percentage) to the sum
of the squares of the observed data (in percentage). This last measure
is an indication of the relative importance of the deviations of model
from data compared with data.

TABLE 4   Observed and Simulated Eye Fixations in Percentages for Runs Not
Included in Tables 2 and 3

Instrument		D. M. Phase I Beginning of Descent		J. F. Phase I Landing Approach	
No.	Name	Data	Model	Data	Model
1	Heading	25.3	22.5	20.5	19.0
3	Air speed	16.9	11.7	10.5	12.0
4	Altimeter	16.9	22.1	6.5	8.2
5 and 6	Pitch and roll	40.0	43.7	24.5	25.8
13	Rate of climb	.9	–	17.0	9.0
14 and 15	Localizer and glide path	–	–	21.0	26.0
	Total	100.0	100.0	100.0	100.0

TABLE 5   Statistical Comparison between Model and Data, Averaged across Instruments

Case Pilot and Phase		Average of Absolute Differences (in percent) between Model and Data	Sum of Squares of Observed Data	Sum of Squares of Differences between Mode and Data	Ratio of Two Preceding Columns
P. M.	I	0.96	2602.50	7.60	.0029
	II	2.60	2925.22	47.26	.0162
	III	3.33	2304.62	104.00	.0451
J. F.	II	2.04	2401.38	28.06	.0117
	III	3.17	1903.00	98.08	.0516
D. M.	I	3.56	2812.12	76.42	.0272
	II	2.28	3075.26	38.32	.0125

Table 6 refers specifically to averages across instruments, giving the above defined indices, averaged across trials, for each individual instrument (or instrument pair); observe that localizer plus glidepath indicator is only pertinent for Phase III (landing approach) of the flight, and, therefore, appears in only two trials. Finally, Table 8 gives the indices globally, first for individual pilots and next for flight phases, averaged in each case over everything else.

The differences between pilots are not really significant. Results for Phase III (landing approach) are poorer than those for the other two phases, beginning of descent and turn, though they are still quite acceptable. This probably reflects the presence of two new signals, as well as some coupling between instruments that may be higher than in the other phases. With respect to accuracy of the model in predicting fixations on particular instruments, rate of climb is the worst. It should be noted that different pilots assign widely different costs to this instrument in relation to others. It is also interesting to note that some of the instruments that have a high degree of information coupling are the three with less accurate predictions, namely rate of climb, air speed, and altimeter, in that order. On the other hand, we have been able to predict distance on pitch and roll quite accurately. This is encouraging since it is the instrument that is observed most frequently.

These results support the basic assumptions involved in the economic queueing model. This model has shown itself capable of

TABLE 6 Statistical Comparison between Model and Data for Individual Instruments Averaged across Pilots and Phases

Instrument No.	Name	No. of Runs Included	Average of Absolute Differences (in percent) between Model and Data	Sum of Squares of Observed Data	Sum of Squares of Differences between Model and Data	Ratio of Two Preceding Columns
1	Heading	7	3.16	3417.79	101.59	.0207
3	Air speed	7	2.27	866.97	54.61	.0630
4	Altimeter	7	2.80	1620.91	70.18	.0433
5 and 6	Pitch and roll	7	1.56	10136.68	27.33	.0027
13	Rate of climb	7	3.04	905.71	119.07	.1310
14–16	Localizer and glide path	2	3.20	1076.04	26.96	.0251

TABLE 7 Statistical Comparison between Model and Data, Overall Results for Pilots and Phases

	No. of Runs Included	Average of Absolute Differences (in percent) between Model and Data	Sum of Squares of Observed Data	Sum of Squares of Differences between Model and Data	Ratio of Two Preceding Columns
Pilot					
P. M.	3	2.36	7832.34	158.86	.0203
J. F.	2	2.65	4304.38	126.14	.0293
D. M.	2	2.92	5887.38	114.74	.0195
Phase					
I–Beginning of descent	2	2.26	5414.62	84.02	.0155
II–Turn	3	2.31	8401.86	113.64	.0135
III–Landing approach	2	3.25	4207.62	202.08	.0480

126 *John W. Senders*

TABLE 8 Comparison of Correlation Coefficients between Data and Model for Nyquist Model (Left) versus Queueing Model (Right)

Pilot	Phase I	II	III
D. M.	.905/.966	.730/.974	–
P. M.	.190/.994	.940/.983	.653/.917
J. F.	–	.903/.984	–.263/.837

accurately representing the behavior of pilots visually sampling their instruments during an instrumented flight. Table 8 presents a comparison of correlation coefficients computed for the fixed Nyquist and the economic queueing models. The queueing model, as can be seen in the table, gives consistently higher correlations. This suggests that there is a trade-off between degree of correlation and complication of conceptualization, which implies that more complex procedures would obtain better results.

GENERAL CONCLUSION AND RECOMMENDATIONS

I have undertaken and completed a program involving extensive instrumentation of a simulator and of the pilots who operate it. The investigation has involved the recording and subsequent transformation of many varieties of data relating to both system and human performance. The basic goals were the testing of models and the examination of the ways in which human operators and system dynamics interact in a more or less deterministic way. The models tested range in sophistication from the very statistical to the very causal. Only some of them could be tested within the framework of the present project, and indeed, as it turned out, some seem to be basically untestable, given the nature of the task presented to the pilot and the kinds of recording and analysis that could be undertaken. Validation in the simulator is limited to two different models of where people look and why they look there when flying on aircraft through a variety of more or less routine maneuvers. One of these models is basically a sampling theorum application, the other an extension of a cyclic queue with the addition of certain cost factors guiding the sampling behavior. In both cases, of course, the signal characteristics have a strong effect on the predictions of the model, so that we would expect both models to relate fairly well to the same body of experimentally obtained data. The results indicate that the statistical predictors are weaker than the queueing model, which depends heavily on individual pilot's estimates of the cost of making certain control activities and the cost of exceeding certain limits. This we might expect. In general, the more detailed the examination of the basis of behavior, the more closely should the model so constructed fit the actuality. The statistical model supposes that eye movements are purely a function of signal frequency characteristics and the desired accuracy of readout. However, because of the nature of instrument displays in which only error signals, i.e., deviations from desired setting, are displayed, it is very difficult to extract ratios of signal power to error power. Instead, these must be inferred. What we have, then, is a fitting of straight lines to the error spectrum to the signal characteristics that governed the pilots' behavior. The results for the three pilots, as presented in Senders *et al.* (1968), show that in all but one case the correlations between the predicted distribution of attention and the observed data are positive and (again, with exception) high. The defect of this model arises from the fact that under certain flight conditions, in particular the final approach, the signal power for certain of the instruments becomes very small and our estimates of the bandwidth of the signal presented rather dubious at best. Thus, our predictions of the attention to be paid to the localizer and glide path during final approach are greatly at variance with the observed behavior of the pilot, as are the estimates of rate-of-turn and rpm. However, for Phase I (beginning of descent) and Phase II (turn) of flight, the correlations are generally high and in the expected direction and suggest that the model has power for predicting the distribution of attention when the pilot is not engaged in effectively continuous control of the signals that he is presented with. [For a complete explanation of the results of this study fitting the model to the data, see Senders *et al.* (1968).]

Where it is possible to use data obtained from pilots to enter into a queueing and cost–effectiveness model, very powerful estimates can be obtained that would be useful for engineering decisions. Where such data cannot be obtained, as for example, in the analysis of sys-

tems that are new and for which no great experience exists, the statistical predictions of the sampling model also yield powerful predictions, although by no means as powerful as those yielded by the
queueing model. In either case, the predictions of these models will
be useful in making estimates of the loading imposed on the pilot by
a well-defined system and in calculating instrument panel configura-
tions based on the way in which people must use the signals that are
to be presented. An interesting application of the principles and
theory that have been developed within this program is presented in
Cobhan (1964). The results of that application appear to support the
general notion that these analyses have immediate and direct engineering utility.

REFERENCES

Carbonell, J. A queueing model of many instrument visual samplings. Trans-
actions on Human Factors in Electronics, AFE-7, 4, 1966.
Cobhan, A. Priority assignment in waiting-line problems. J. Oper. Res. Soc. Am.,
2, 70–76, 1964.
Jones, R. E., J. L. Milton, and P. M. Fitts. Eye Fixations of Aircraft Pilots: A
Review of Prior Eye-Movement Studies and a Description of a Technique for
Recording the Frequency, Duration and Sequence of Eye Fixations during
Instrument Flight. USAF Tech. Report 5837 (AT I 65996), 1946.
Lindquist, H., and R. Gross. Human Engineering Man–Machine Study of a
Weapon System. Minneapolis-Honeywell Aero. Report R-ED 6094, Minn.-
Honeywell, Mineapolis, Minn., 1958.
Senders, J. W. Man's capacity to use information from complex displays. Infor-
mation Theory in Psychology. The Free Press, Glencoe, Ill., 1955.
Senders, J. W. Information Input Rates to Human Users: Recent Research
Results. W.A.D.C. Symposium on Air Force Flight Instrumentation Pro-
gram. Wright-Patterson AFB, Ohio, 1968.
Senders, J. W. The Human Operator as a Monitor and Controller of Multi-degree
of Freedom Systems. IEEE, Trans. on Human Factors in Electronics, HFE-S,
1, 1964.
Senders, J. W. A Re-analysis of the Pilot Eye-Movement Data. Trans. on Human
Factors in Electronics, IEEE, HFE-7, 2, 1966.
Senders, J. W., J. J. Elkind, M. C. Grignetti, and R. Smallwood. An Investigation
of the Visual Sampling Behavior of Human Observers. BBN Report 1681,
1965.
Senders, J. W., J. R. Carbonell, and J. W. Ward. Human Visual Sampling; a Simulation Validation Study. BBN Report 1246, 1968.
Smallwood, R. Internal Models and the Human Instrument Monitor. Symposium
on Human Factors in Electronics, IEEE, Mineapolis, Minn., 1966.

RALPH N. HABER
UNIVERSITY OF ROCHESTER

Visual Information Storage

Although educational psychologists have studied reading and reading disabilities extensively, they have not usually thought of reading as a process that depends on multistaged extraction of information from briefly fixated symbolic stimuli. On the other hand, some recent work by experimental psychologists with basic interests in perception and memory have led to new concepts and methods of great potential value. I particularly want to mention the work done by Sperling (1967), Hochberg (1970), Neisser (1967), Kolers (1970), Sternberg (1969), Posner (1967), and Bryden (1967), though I am forced to do many injustices to others by presenting such a short list.

These men have all focused on one or more of the information extraction processes involved in recognizing, identifying, matching, or otherwise responding to linguistic stimuli. Their assumption, in one form or another, is that during each fixation or presentation, a number of discrete processes occur, each of which can be identified by proper experimental operations. Taken together, this work has

*The research from my laboratory reported here was supported in part by research grants from the United States Public Health Service (MH 10753), and from the National Science Foundation (GB 5910 and GB 4547). This paper was completed while the author held a special postdoctoral fellowship from the United States Public Health Service (MH 24765) at the Medical Research Council's Applied Psychology Unit at Cambridge, England.

suggested to me a general model concerning the early stages of these processes, a model that has been guiding my thinking for some time now. While not specifically attributing any part of this model to any of these theorists, let me describe some of the model's principal components, represented in four stages.

The first stage of the model assumes that the patterned excitation formed on each retina is coded as a set of distinctive visual features by the receptive field organization of each retinal–neural system. The features available probably include only contour, line, angle, orientation, motion, retinal disparity, and color, although it is possible that detectors of other features will be discovered for the human visual system. Thus, the first processing stage is a transduction from the patterned optical array, distributed in space and time on the two retinal surfaces, into a set of coded features. It is specifically assumed that this sensory encoding of features is uninfluenced by memory, set, expectation, or any type of prior experience with the stimulus. Thus, the same mapping of features is found in a visually experienced or a naïve perceiver. However, the mapping is highly sensitive to the adaptive state of the eyes and to the specific parts of the retinal surfaces on which the stimulus falls. [See Blakemore and Campbell (1969) for an excellent example of a detailed study of the properties of visual feature extraction processes in human visual perception.]

The result of this first stage is a set of primitive features that are transmitted and represented centrally in a visual feature storage (Stage II). I assume that this storage is what Sperling (1960) rediscovered and named "visual information storage" and what Neisser (1967) has called "iconic storage." The features are present in this storage as long as the optical array from the stimulus falls on the retinas. The features persist briefly after the stimulus terminates or the eye position changes by means of saccadic movements to register a new stimulus pattern. The duration of the persistence is about the same as the typical fixation time for free viewing or reading, on the order of ¼–½ sec. This time will tend to minimize the amount of overlap of successive icons, since I assume that if a second stimulus is presented while the features of the first are still in storage, the two icons will combine so that under most circumstances a separate processing of the features from the two stimuli will become more difficult, if not impossible.

The content of Stage II is a set of features that, while already coded, are themselves not yet in a form familiar to the perceiver. Hochberg (1968, 1970) has stressed this point most emphatically. We see in a single glance only those features of the stimulus that are centrally represented. To achieve a perception of a meaningful pattern, several glances are usually needed, and, even more important, some type of schematic or cognitive structure needs to guide the combination or construction of features within and between glances into familiar forms and patterns. Thus, Stage III consists of another transduction of information, this time from the primitive visual features in Stage II iconic storage into constructions of patterns following schematic rules or programs of organization based on prior experience, set, expectation, and other concomitant sensory information. These programs will differ depending on the stimuli or, rather, upon what the perceiver expects the stimuli to be. Thus, if he is expecting linguistic patterns (e.g., letters of words in sentences), then one set of programs is activated to transfer the features. If he expects to see faces or landscapes or the view through the windshield of a moving car, then the constructions are quite different and follow rules of very different kinds of programs.

Stage IV contains the results of the operations of the schematic programs. For linguistic material, this has generally been called short-term memory and is probably initially in the form of acoustic representations. For pictorial stimuli, it may be called a visual image of the stimulus or what Richardson (1969) more appropriately calls a memory image, for most perceivers at least. The fidelity of the details of this representation to the original pattern in the optical array depends on the program used to construct the representation. How long the perceiver will remember the stimulus and his ease of retrieving it for recall or recognition will also depend on the program, the amount and redundancy of information contained in the construction, and the relationship to other constructions presently being made or maintained in memory.

Further transductions to more permanent representation (e.g., to long-term memory) presumably also occur, though these are presently of somewhat less concern to me than to researchers working more exclusively with models of memory [e.g., see most of the papers in Norman (1970)].

Having briefly sketched this model or guide, I would like to describe some recent experimental work from my laboratory that concerns two different aspects of this general model. The first aspect is the nature of the Stage II visual representation, and the second is the extraction and processing of information from Stage II (what I have called Stage III). These studies also raise methodological and operational questions of some interest.

Most of the evidence suggesting that there is an iconic storage has been indirect, since it is based on the amount of information the subject has available after the supposed icon has faded. I wanted to develop some more direct tests, ones that ask the perceiver to describe some properties of his icon while it is still present.

Lionel Standing, while a Research Associate at the University of Rochester for 2 years, conducted several experiments with me on this problem. The difficulty we faced was that the icon is too brief for us to ask the subject to tell us how long it persisted. With suitable adjustment in intensity, for example, flashes of 10^{-9} sec can appear to be just as long as flashes of 10^{-2} sec, a difference of 7 log units, which suggests that we could not rely on judgments of absolute duration. We explored three alternative procedures, ones that also avoided the indirect partial report measurements.

One procedure (Haber and Standing, 1969) involved recycling a light flash. As an analogy, imagine that you are to operate an incandescent lamp with the instruction to turn it on momentarily, then quickly off, and then on again as soon as it appears to have completely faded—several seconds for most incandescent lights—and imagine that you repeat this procedure a number of times. If a timer is attached to the light switch, the resultant pattern of on–off intervals will show that you turned the switch on briefly every several seconds. The interval between the on-switchings would be a measure of the visual persistence of the filament in the light bulb plus whatever persistence there might be in the measuring instrument—your eye. We conducted this same experiment, except that we used a light that had a negligible persistence (only a few microseconds). Consequently, any apparent persistence would be in the eye and not in the light. Figure 1 illustrates this procedure. A black outline figure on a white background was presented in one channel of a tachistoscope for 10–20 msec, followed by a variable off-time in which a blank, white adaptation field replaced the stimulus field. These two channels continued to alternate for a number of cycles. The subject's task was to watch the two fields and decide whether the black outline form completely faded or disappeared after each of its flashes or whether it persisted until it came on again. If the subject said it had disappeared, then the interflash interval was shortened until a point was located for which it had just disappeared. Following appropriate psychophysical procedures, we could then determine the persistence of the visual form. Figure 2 shows the results over several conditions based on 10 subjects. When the subject is adapted to a fairly high level of illumination (as when reading), ¼ sec must be interposed between each flash for the subject to say that the flash had just faded. Cutting the amount of light by two log units only slightly increases the persistence. Dark-adapting the subject, on the other hand, by turning off the adaptation field nearly doubles the persistence, an effect comparable to that of the partial report measures of iconic storage (Sperling, 1960). Hence, it seems that persistence is not very dependent on level of illumination but that it is highly dependent upon adaptation-level.

In another condition, we presented alternate flashes dichoptically to the eyes. If the persistence is entirely retinal, that is, both generated and monitored by the subject retinally, then the flashes to each eye would have to come 250 msec apart for the subject to say that the figure had just faded. Since only every other flash comes to the same eye, the overall rate of flashing would have to be doubled. On the other hand, if the persistence is measured centrally then no

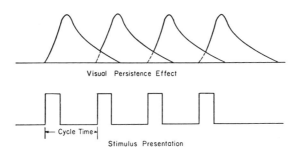

FIGURE 1   Procedure illustrating the recycling of a light flash of a few microseconds persistence.

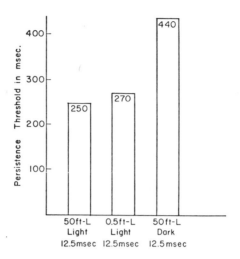

Stimulus presentation of a black circle

FIGURE 2   Results of the recycling of a light
flash of a few microseconds' persistence over
several conditions based on 10 subjects.

change in the rate of flashing would be needed even with dichoptic
presentations. The central hypothesis was strongly supported since
the dichoptic presentations required the same rate. Thus, while the
persistence may be generated retinally, though there is no reason to
assume that it is, the perceiver's judgment of the persistence must be
occurring at some point after the information from the two eyes has
been combined.

We have used this experimental design with a number of other
stimuli, including both rare and familiar words (Standing *et al.,*
1969). The effects have been virtually identical with both types of
words, which suggests that the content of the stimulus or its meaning-
fulness is not relevant to its persistence.

A second procedure to investigate visual storage was initially
worked out by Haber and Nathanson (1968) and extended by Haber
and Standing (1969). The subject was instructed to look at an outline
figure (e.g., a camel) that he viewed through a vertical slit 1/8 in.
wide that moved back and forth in front of the figure. Thus, at any
instant, only a small fraction of the figure was on view, that which

could be seen through the slit. In this procedure, the subject tended to fixate some particular part of the figure, and if the slit was set in very rapid oscillatory motion, such that, for example, only 50 msec elapsed from the time the left edge of the figure appeared until the right edge of the figure was exposed, then the figure has been painted across the retina in only 50 msec. Subjects universally report that they can see the entire figure and that its contours are fairly sharp in this condition. The faster the slit is set in motion, the darker the contours, approaching the sharpness of the perceived contours when the figure is seen in its entirety.

The experimental procedure was to vary the speed of oscillation and ask the subject at each speed whether the entire figure could be seen or whether, while one end was sharply in view because the slit had just swept over it, the other end of the figure had faded from view. Following a psychophysical procedure similar to that in the previous experiment, we determined the speed of oscillation necessary for the subject to say that the entire figure just remained in view without part of it fading while another part was sharp. This duration for 10 subjects was about 280 msec under normal room illumination. It increased to 300 msec in very dim illumination. Thus, these estimates of iconic persistence are virtually the same as those found in the recycling procedure.

A third experimental procedure that we have used (Haber and Standing, 1970) follows a design initially suggested by Sperling (1967). The subject observes a flash of light. Coincident with its onset, he hears a very brief click. The subject is told that every few seconds he will again see and hear the paired flash–click. Between the presentations of each pair the subject is free to adjust a timer that will change the relative asynchrony of the flash and click, so that if he judges that the click came before the flash, he can delay the click relative to the flash. The subject views the pairs enough times to match the simultaneity of the onsets satisfactorily. Then the click is set to occur near the offset of the flash, and the subject is again asked to make a series of judgments until he has set the click to be apparently simultaneous with the offset of the flash. Figure 3 illustrates the experimental design. Our assumption is that the interclick interval calculated from these two sets of judgments would be an index of the apparent duration of the stimulus, includ-

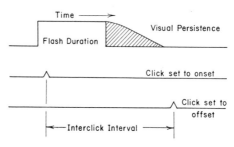

Persistence = Interclick Interval - Flash Duration

FIGURE 3   Illustration of an experimental
procedure in which the subject hears a click
coincident with the observation of a flashed
light. A timer is used by the subject to match
the simultaneity of the flash–click onsets.

ing any persistence. If there is no persistence at all, that is, if the
subject thinks the stimulus terminates simultaneously with its physical termination, then the interclick interval should equal the duration
of the stimulus. On the other hand, if the subject feels that a 50 msec
stimulus persisted for 200 msec after it was physically turned off, he
should set the interclick interval at 250 msec. Our subjects, after
some practice, found this a relatively easy series of judgments to
make because they noted that when they felt the click and the flash
just coincided, they also had a feeling of apparent causality between
the two. Once this perception occurred, the standard deviation of
the judgments was very small.

Figure 4 reports results for various conditions of light and dark
adaptation. Here the results are slightly different from those of the
previous studies. If the flash is very brief, under 30 or 40 msec, the
light-adapted subject adds a persistence of nearly 200 msec (bottom
function), and the dark-adapted subject nearly 400 msec (top function). However, if the flash is longer, the amount of persistence is
much less until, by the time the flash is itself ¼ to ½ sec, the amount
of persistence becomes negligible. Hence, only brief flashes appear
to have any persistence. This finding becomes important to my later
discussion. For those brief flashes, the amount of persistence, as
measured in this third procedure, is shown to be quite close to the
estimates based on the other two and on the indirect procedures.

One further question was investigated in this study. Sperling (1963) and Averbach and Coriell (1961) argued that iconic storage should be erasable. A number of mechanisms have been proposed for this type of process, the most parsimonious one being that a subsequent stimulus creates its own icon, which replaces the icon of the previous stimulation. This is discussed in some detail by Neisser (1967). Since we were concerned with the visual characteristics of iconic storage, we included a condition in which a visual masking noise followed the display after various delays. Figure 5 shows the results for the light-adapted condition. Since the parameter in the figure is the interval from the onset of the stimulus until the onset of the masking noise, it is clear that the onset of the masking noise

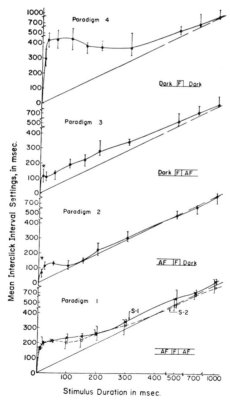

FIGURE 4   Results for various conditions of light and dark adaptation.

terminates the persistence rather precisely, since all of the points
tend to fall along straight lines of zero slope. Only those values corresponding to persistences that have already faded deviate from this
result. Since brief flashes have a persistence of just less than 200 msec,
if the masking noise arrives after 200 msec, the persistence has ended
by itself, and the subject will set the interclick interval at less than
the interval between the onset of the stimulus and the onset of the
masking noise. What is most noteworthy is that there are no excep-
tions to the general principle that the visual noise mask will termi-
nate the persistence of a stimulus if the mask arrives before the
normal persistence is ended of its own accord. If the persistence
has ended, the mask can have no effect on it.

Since the experiments just reviewed all require the subject to
report some visual characteristic of iconic storage, it must be that
he can see something in his icon—it is a *visual* persistence. Perhaps,
it might be interesting to speculate as to what it is that the subject

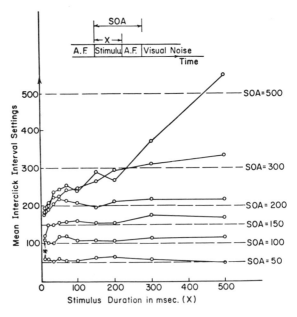

FIGURE 5   Results of a procedure under a light-adapted
condition where a visual masking noise followed a display
after various delays.

sees. The experiments just reviewed do not tell us much about this. In terms of the general model being presented here, however, I suggest that he does not know what he sees. By that I mean that he can tell that there is something out there, but at that time he has not performed any analysis integration, construction, or labeling, so that the material is uncoded, unidentified, unrecognized, and unfamiliar. A frequent comment made by subjects in all of our experiments concerns the unknowability of brief inputs. If the stimulus is terminated abruptly by visual noise but had been bright and had good contrast, subjects will say that they saw the stimulus clearly but that they did not have enough time to recognize it.

To show this more explicitly, we performed one experiment (Haber and Standing, 1968) in which the subject was asked to rate the clarity (that is, the sharpness of the contrast) of some letters that were briefly presented on some of the trials. On other trials he was asked to recognize the letters. The letters were presented for a fixed duration, which would have been adequate for a high clarity-rating and for near-perfect recognition if they had not been followed by visual noise. However, visual noise followed the display after a variable delay. We found that for very brief delay-intervals the subject would report that the clarity had already achieved a high level, even though in the other condition at the same interval he was unable to recognize the letters much above chance. Hence, we demonstrated experimentally that they could see the letters clearly but were unable to recognize them. Liss (1969) has reported a similar effect.

While these experiments raise as many questions as they answer, they do lend strong support to the supposition that there is a visual representation of information (Stage II in the model), one that begins when the stimulus begins and persists very briefly after the stimulus ends. I will now shift to some studies of the processing of information contained in this representation (Stage III). The research design followed in my experiments, as well as in many others, involves presenting a single brief flash of an array of information, usually linguistic material, and controlling the time the subject has available to process that information by following the array with a field of visual noise.

This research strategy was developed most recently by Sperling (1963). He briefly presented an array of letters and asked the subject

to report the letters he saw, guessing if necessary. Immediately following the array was a visual noise field made up of a random arrangement of lines and curves superimposed over the position where the
array had been. Sperling found a linear relationship between the exposure duration of the array and the number of letters correctly reported, with a slope of one letter per 10 msec (see Figure 6). From
this he argued that the subject requires 10 msec to process each letter,
which he does serially, scanning one item at a time from left to right.
While the serial aspect of the interpretation of the results is not supported by later data, including Sperling (1967), the major importance
of the study was the use of visual noise to control the time available
for processing the information contained in the stimuli. I will add
some further comments about this procedure after I have reviewed
some experimental data from my laboratory.

We have just completed two varieties of replications of the Sperling (1963) design (Haber *et al.*, in preparation). In each, arrays of

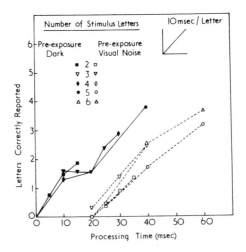

FIGURE 6   Presentation of Sperling's research strategy in which an array of letters
is briefly displayed and the subject reports
what he sees. Immediately following the
array is a visual noise field composed of a
random arrangement of lines and curves
superimposed over the position where the
array had been.

one, two, three, and four letters were flashed. The subject reported the letters he saw, guessing if necessary. Visual noise followed the array by a variable delay. The time from the onset of the array to the onset of the visual noise operationally defines the time available for processing the letters in the array. The subjects, initially naïve, were tested over 15 days in the first study and tested up to 40 days in the second study.

During the first few days of practice in the first experiment, each subject needed about 60 msec of processing time to report one letter, 70 for two, 80 for three, and nearly 100 for four letters. Assuming that 50 msec were needed before processing began (an assumption examined below), these results correspond closely to those of Sperling's, except for the longer time needed to begin processing. However, after 12 days of practice the functions have converged so that even four letters can be reported with 60 msec of processing time (see Figure 7).

It appears as though a serial processing strategy were being used by the unpracticed subject, who then switches to the parallel strategy (processing several letters at a time) as he becomes more experienced. However, the data showing the serial position of the letters suggest otherwise, for two important reasons. Although the subject always does better for letters on the left as compared to those on the right, even when he is less than perfect on a left-hand letter he already is correctly reporting some of the right-hand letters. Thus, he must have been processing more than one letter at a time. This is shown in Figure 8 for four-letter arrays. The results for smaller arrays mirror this one closely. Further, the subject always does better for any particular letter position when more letters are contained in the array. Thus, he does better on the first letter in a two-letter array than he does for a one-letter array. Figure 9 illustrates this finding for the first letter of the four different sizes of arrays. This result could not be explained by sequential dependencies, since the stimuli are zero-order approximations to English. Again it suggests that the subject is processing more than one letter at a time. These effects are equally true before and after practice.

In the second replication we manipulated the ratio of the array duration (on-time) to the duration of the interval between the offset of the array and the onset of the visual noise (off-time). Because we

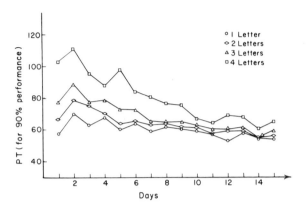

FIGURE 7   A replication of the Sperling design in which
subjects after 12 days of practice are able to lessen the
processing time of reporting four letters from almost
100 msec to 60 msec.

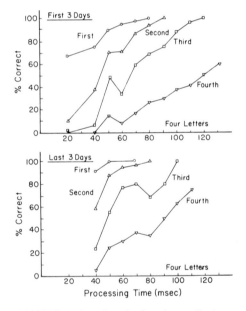

FIGURE 8   Results of a four-letter display
indicating the switch from serial to parallel
processing by a subject as he becomes experienced. A better score for recognition of
left-hand letters is observed.

used a lower background luminance, processing began faster. However, once the array was on for 10 to 20 msec, all ratios of on-to-off-time produced the same level of accuracy. Hence processing time is the critical independent variable and not the exposure duration, except when the latter is so brief that the features in the stimulus never become represented in the iconic storage.

These results suggest that processing probably proceeds from left to right but not in a simple item-by-item serial order. The rate of 10 msec per item can only characterize an overall rate and cannot be used to describe the scanning and processing itself. Unfortunately, these studies do not tell us whether the subject might be processing several letters at a time or whether he is scanning the whole array from left to right a number of times, completing the processing of one letter per scan. It should be noted that Sperling (1967) also rejected his earlier serial model on the basis of serial position data similar to those reported here. He too, however, had no evidence on how to describe a process that could have accounted for the data.

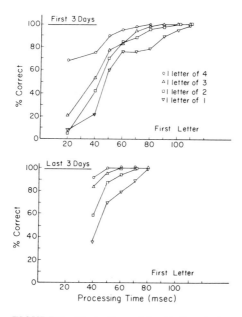

FIGURE 9   Illustration of the finding that a subject does better on reporting the first letter in four different sizes of arrays.

In another study (Haber and Nathanson, 1969) we looked at processing time as an independent variable for sequential presentation of
letters, rather than presentation of all of the letters in a single flash.
We assumed that the arrival of the second letter in the same retinal
location as the first acts to stop the processing of the first letter, and
likewise for each subsequent letter. The processing time for each
letter can then be specified as the time from the onset of a letter
until the onset of the next letter. This is the sum of the letter duration plus the time from the offset of one letter to the onset of the
next letter. We varied processing time and stimulus duration inde-
pendently by variation of the off-time between letters. Four subjects
were tested, each of whom saw 1,250 frequent English words, sub-
divided into five lengths (four, five, six, seven, or eight letters), five
on-times (10, 25, 50, 100, and 150 msec), and five similiar off-times.
Thus, the shortest processing time per letter was 20 msec and the
longest, 300 msec. The subject pressed a button that initiated the
sequence. He reported the letters that he was sure he saw (not
guessed) as soon as the last letter ended.

We found that the ratio of on-time to off-time could be varied
as much as 15:1 without changing the performance for every on–off
combination with the same total processing time. The only predictor
of the number of letters correctly reported was the duration of processing time. This was true for each S and for each word length. This
finding supports the notion that it is the time available to process the
stimulus controlled by a subsequent event and not merely the duration of the stimulus alone that is the proper independent variable in
information processing experiments.

An interesting and, on the surface, surprising finding was the very
long processing times required for the subject to report each letter
correctly in the sequential presentation procedure. Not until the
processing times exceeded 200 to 250 msec per letter was the subject
able to report all of the letters nearly perfectly. As is clear from the
studies described earlier, that much time would have permitted a
report of at least four letters and perhaps as many as 10 to 20 letters
when they were presented simultaneously. Presenting a small amount
of information in one fixation or flash does not mean that another
small amount can be presented sooner in time. I think that the sequential rate of fixation in reading—about 250 msec—represents

about the minimum sequential rate for any information processing task, quite independent of how much or how little information had been presented. I think it is no coincidence that the persistence from briefly flashed stimuli extends the effective stimulus to around ¼ sec. If the stimulus does not last that long, it is extended, but there is no persistence to extend a longer stimulus. Thus, this mechanism appears to guarantee at least ¼ sec of processing time.

The last experiment I want to mention (Lorinstein and Haber, in preparation) used the Sperling visual noise design but with nonlinguistic material. The display consisted of 1 to 16 dots, each of which occupied one of 64 possible locations in an 8 X 8 matrix. The subject was instructed to count, not estimate, the number of dots that had been presented. The duration of the display was 20 msec—long enough to count up to 10 dots easily without error when no visual noise followed the display. The visual noise field, consisting of larger dots in all 64 locations, followed the display by a variable interval. We found strong evidence for a serial processing of the dots. For each 4 msec that the visual noise was delayed (beyond an initial 45 msec needed to begin processing), one more dot could be counted, up to about six dots (see Figure 10 for the data on three subjects). Beyond six dots the counting appeared to slow down dramatically, though this could have been due to spatial factors.

The converging operations in support of a serial processing interpretation are much less ambiguous than those from the studies with linguistic stimuli. For example, if counting is serial and takes, say, 4 msec per dot to perform, then giving a processing time of 65 msec (including the 45 msec needed to begin counting) should permit the subject to count five dots, regardless of the number greater than that presented. The upper part of Figure 11 shows best-fitted functions for three subjects combined. These strongly support the argument that the subject will count all of the dots for which he has processing time available.

In a second condition in the same experiment, we did not use visual noise, but we varied the exposure duration of the display from 20 msec to 4 msec. This range was chosen so that at the lower level some of the dots would not be seen due to their inadequate contrast. We tested this condition to compare it with the visual noise condition in order to test more explicitly whether visual noise restricted the

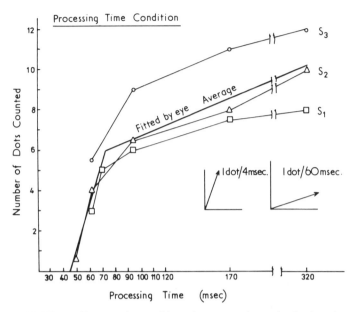

FIGURE 10   Data on three subjects in an experiment by Lorinstein and Haber using the Sperling visual noise design but with nonlinguistic material.

time available to process the dots or only reduced the clarity of the dots, making them more difficult to see and, hence, to count. The results in the second condition were quite different from the first (see the bottom portion of Figure 11). The different durations produced linear functions that generally started at the origin and rose with their slope determined by the duration: The higher the duration, the higher the proportion of dots in each display that was counted. Hence, lower durations appear to make some dots uncountable because the subject cannot see them, while visual noise appears to restrict the time available to count the dots, all of which would have been countable otherwise.

The experiments focusing on Stage III represent a rather cursory glance at the kinds of research on extraction of information that I have been carrying out in my laboratory. Again, they raise more questions than they answer, although some of their implications are becoming clear. By way of conclusion I would like to comment on several of those nagging questions: (1) How reasonable is it to use single tachistoscopic flashes to stimulate the processing of information that occurs during separate fixations while reading? (2) How much can be generalized from the widespread use of *nonmeaningful* linguistic stimuli in tachistoscopic experiments? (3) What can be said about serial models of information processing? (4) Is the operational definition of processing time through manipulation of the delay of visual noise proving useful?

I have been using tachistoscopic presentations as a way to simulate what a reader might see during a single fixation. In some sense this is like trying to read during a lightening storm. It is obviously a weak analogy in the sense that readers make multiple fixations as part of a sequential process. On the other hand, through the use of visual noise as somewhat analogous to the effects imposed by the next fixation, the time available to process the content of the information seen in a single fixation can be studied in some detail. This is especially useful to uncover the microgenetic nature of the processing, since these experiments have all made it much more obvious how many separable processes can be uncovered, even within a single presentation or fixation.

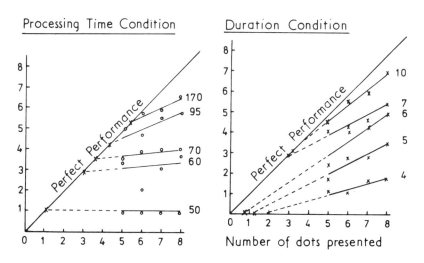

FIGURE 11   Upper portion shows the effect of varying processing time on mean number of dots counted. The lower portion shows the effect of varying the duration of the display.

But we cannot stop here. Many more experiments must compare the interpretations drawn from single presentations to those from sequential presentations or successive fixation experiments. Previously, I mentioned briefly that I see an important commonality between the ¼-sec effective stimulus duration brought about by the persistence mechanism and the typical duration of each fixation in reading. I think that with further research we shall find that all of the information in linguistic presentations can be extracted in ¼ sec and that allowing more time will make no further improvement in this type of processing task. Further, I think I already have enough data to argue that most of the 250 msec is spent in processing the representation of the display and does not require the display to be on view all of that time. I would estimate that, in reading, no more than 50 msec of the fixation time is needed for stimulus reception under normal room illumination. As long as the next fixation is delayed sufficiently to permit processing to occur, actual viewing time can be short.

The second point concerns the rather typical use of nonsense material for tachistoscopic display experiments, such as nearly all of those discussed in this paper. This is done in order to simplify the interpretation of the subject's responses. If the subject reports a letter of a zero-order approximation to an English word, we can be sure that he saw that letter, rather than merely anticipated it on the basis of his knowledge of sequential dependencies. Of course the problem is that a subject has learned to use such dependencies and these play a critical role in information processing skills such as used in reading. It seems obvious to me that, as readers, we never process each letter. We probably do not even process evey word, especially when reading simple or predictable material. The processing strategies, schemes, or programs used to construct the meaning out of print must be very different from those demanded for use when nonwords are presented, for in the latter situation every letter must be looked at since no constructed meaning is possible beyond the letter names.

This brings me to my third comment, concerning the evidence for serial processing. I do not think these experiments with nonmeaningful material are very relevant to the question of whether processing in reading is serial. Although they can tell us a great deal about the processing done in this fairly atypical material and task, we need to

be much more careful about applying generalizations from this research to the types of tasks and skills we spent most of our time
performing. Thus, while Sperling's experiment in 1963 and its replications suggest a left-to-right but multiple-letter scan, I feel we
must be very cautious in arguing that this does or does not apply
to reading as well. Given our present state of knowledge, I think such
a generalization is probably appropriate, especially concerning the
left-to-right scanning. But we must test this both with meaningful
material and in multiple-fixation processing tasks. Until this is done,
we can only generalize to the processing of nonsense words.

Finally, a number of other researchers as well as myself are placing
heavy reliance on the use of visual noise to control the time available
for processing. Several of the experiments have permitted tests of
some of the assumptions underlying this operational definition,
especially as contrasted to an interpretation that stresses the contrast reduction effects on the display caused by the visual masking
noise. I have commented on this evidence briefly here and in much
greater detail elsewhere (Haber, 1968, 1969a, b, 1970; Haber
and Standing, 1970). While the issue is by no means settled, I feel
that the evidence comfortably supports continued use of this technique to permit simulation of a separate fixation by a tachistoscopic
presentation.

In summary, I have briefly presented a general information processing model. Within its context I have presented some evidence of
visual representations and persistence of briefly viewed stimuli and
of how information is extracted in such representations. A number
of theoretical and methodological issues have been discussed.

REFERENCES

Averbach, M., and A. S. Coriell. Short-term memory in vision. Bell Syst. Tech.
    J., 40, 309–328, 1961.
Blakemore, C., and F. W. Campbell. On the existence of neurones in the human
    visual system selectively sensitive to the orientation and size of retinal images.
    J. Phys., 203, 237–260, 1969.
Bryden, M. P. A model for the sequential organization of behavior. Can. J.
    Psych., 21, 37–56, 1967.
Haber, R. N. A replication and extension of the Eriksen & Steffey (1964) ex-
    periment on short term visual memory. Percept. Psychophys. 4, 341–343,
    1968.

Haber, R. N. Information processing analysis of visual perception: An intro-
duction, 1–15. In R. N. Haber, ed., Information Processing Approaches to
Visual Perception. New York, Holt, Rinehart and Winston, 1969a.

Haber, R. N. Repetition, visual persistence, visual noise, and information processing, 121–140. In K. N. Leibovic, ed., Information Processing in the
Nervous System. New York, Springer-Verlag Publishing Co., 1969b.

Haber, R. N. A note on how to choose a mask. Physch. Bull., 74, 373–376, 1970.

Haber, R. N., and L. S. Nathanson. Post-retinal storage?–Parks' camel as seen
through the eye of a needle. Percept. Psychophys., 3, 349–355, 1968.

Haber, R. N., and L. S. Nathanson. Processing of sequentially presented letters.
Percept. Psychophys. 5, 359–361, 1969.

Haber, R. N., and L. G. Standing. Clarity and recognition of masked and degraded stimuli. Psychonomic Sci., 13, 83–84, 1968.

Haber, R. N., and L. G. Standing. Direct measures of short-term visual storage.
Q. J. Exp. Psych., 21, 43–56, 1969.

Haber, R. N., and L. G. Standing. Direct estimates of apparent duration of a flash
followed by visual noise. Can. J. Psych., 24, 216–229, 1970.

Haber, R. N., L. G. Standing, and J. Boss. Processing of letter information from
brief visual displays. In preparation.

Hochberg, J. In the mind's eye, 309–331. In R. N. Haber, ed., Contemporary
Theory and Research in Visual Perception, New York, Holt, Rinehart and
Winston, 1968.

Hochberg, J. Attention, organization and consciousness, 99–124. In D. Mostofsky,
ed., Attention: Contemporary Theory and Analysis. New York, Appleton-
Century-Croft, 1970.

Kolers, P. A. Three stages in reading, 90–118. In H. Levin and J. Williams, eds.,
Basic Studies in Reading, New York, Basic Books, 1970.

Liss, P. Does backward masking by visual noise stop stimulus processing? Percept. Psychophys., 4, 328–330, 1969.

Lorinstein, I. B., and R. N. Haber. Counting dots of masked and degraded
presentations. In preparation.

Neisser, U. Cognitive Psychology. New York, Appleton-Century-Croft, 1967.

Norman, D. A. Models of Human Memory. New York, Academic Press, 1970.

Posner, M. I. Short term memory systems in human information processing.
Acta Psychol. 27, 267–284, 1967.

Richardson, A. Mental Imagery. New York, Springer, 1969.

Sperling, G. The information available in brief visual presentations. Psych.
Monogr., 74 (Whole No. 498), 1–29, 1960.

Sperling. G. A model for visual memory tasks. Hum. Factors, 5, 19–31, 1963.

Sperling, G. Successive approximations to a model for short-term memory.
Acta Psychol., 23, 285–292, 1967.

Sternberg, S. Mental scanning: Some evidence from reaction time experiments.
Am. Sci., 57, 1969.

Standing, L. G., R. N. Haber, M. Cataldo, and B. D. Sales. Two types of short-
term visual storage. Percept. Psychophys., 5, 193–196, 1969.